THE DREYFUS AFFAIR

Tragedy of Errors?

PROBLEMS IN EUROPEAN CIVILIZATION

UNDER THE EDITORIAL DIRECTION OF
Ralph W. Greenlaw* and Dwight E. Lee†

DECLINE AND FALL OF THE ROMAN EMPIRE — WHY DID IT COLLAPSE? †

THE PIRENNE THESIS — ANALYSIS, CRITICISM, AND REVISION*

THE CORONATION OF CHARLEMAGNE — WHAT DID IT SIGNIFY? *

THE GREGORIAN EPOCH — REFORMATION, REVOLUTION, REACTION? *

INNOCENT III — VICAR OF CHRIST OR LORD OF THE WORLD? †

THE RENAISSANCE — MEDIEVAL OR MODERN? *

MACHIAVELLI — CYNIC, PATRIOT, OR POLITICAL SCIENTIST? *

THE REFORMATION — MATERIAL OR SPIRITUAL? *

THE CHARACTER OF PHILIP II — THE PROBLEM OF MORAL JUDGMENTS IN HISTORY*

PROTESTANTISM AND CAPITALISM — THE WEBER THESIS AND ITS CRITICS*

THE ORIGINS OF THE ENGLISH CIVIL WAR — CONSPIRACY, CRUSADE, OR CLASS
    CONFLICT? *

THE REVOLUTION OF 1688 — WHIG TRIUMPH OR PALACE REVOLUTION? †

PETER THE GREAT — REFORMER OR REVOLUTIONARY? †

THE GREATNESS OF LOUIS XIV — MYTH OR REALITY? *

THE EIGHTEENTH-CENTURY REVOLUTION — FRENCH OR WESTERN? †

THE ECONOMIC ORIGINS OF THE FRENCH REVOLUTION — POVERTY OR PROSPERITY? *

METTERNICH, THE "COACHMAN OF EUROPE" — STATESMAN OR EVIL GENIUS? *

THE INDUSTRIAL REVOLUTION IN BRITAIN — TRIUMPH OR DISASTER? *

1848 — A TURNING POINT? *

NAPOLEON III — BUFFOON, MODERN DICTATOR, OR SPHINX? †

OTTO VON BISMARCK — A HISTORICAL ASSESSMENT*

THE "NEW IMPERIALISM" — ANALYSIS OF LATE NINETEENTH-CENTURY EXPANSION*

THE DREYFUS AFFAIR — A TRAGEDY OF ERRORS? †

THE OUTBREAK OF THE FIRST WORLD WAR — WHO WAS RESPONSIBLE? *

THE RUSSIAN REVOLUTION AND BOLSHEVIK VICTORY — WHY AND HOW? *

THE VERSAILLES SETTLEMENT — WAS IT DOOMED TO FAILURE? *

THE ETHIOPIAN CRISIS — TOUCHSTONE OF APPEASEMENT? *

THE NAZI REVOLUTION — GERMANY'S GUILT OR GERMANY'S FATE? *

THE BRITISH IN INDIA — IMPERIALISM OR TRUSTEESHIP? †

THE OUTBREAK OF THE SECOND WORLD WAR — DESIGN OR BLUNDER? †

THE COLD WAR — IDEOLOGICAL CONFLICT OR POWER STRUGGLE? †

Other volumes in preparation

PROBLEMS IN EUROPEAN CIVILIZATION

THE
DREYFUS AFFAIR

Tragedy of Errors?

EDITED WITH AN INTRODUCTION BY

Leslie Derfler

CARNEGIE INSTITUTE OF TECHNOLOGY

D. C. HEATH AND COMPANY · BOSTON

Table of Contents

v

Introduction

THE Dreyfus Affair was technically and legally the trial, conviction, and punishment of a French army officer on the charge of selling military secrets to the German government; the subsequent reopening of the case, his retrial, reconviction, and immediate pardon; and later, still another reopening and review with the complete vindication of the accused. All this took twelve years.

The Affair, however, can be considered in a number of ways. The long and difficult struggle of the early Dreyfusards to expose the one they believed to be the real culprit makes the most thrilling and fantastic of detective stories. The division across existing alignments of almost all France into two hostile camps — those who demanded revision of the case and those determined to prevent it, those who attached supreme value to justice for the individual and those who would subordinate him to the best interests of the state — provides perhaps the perfect, certainly the clearest, case history of the moral crisis undergone by a nation. We have, furthermore, a now classic illustration of the battle for supremacy waged within a republic between its civil and military powers, as well as the plainest presentation of the arguments used by both sides. From an intellectual and literary point of view, the Affair served at the turn of the century as the experience of an entire generation. Finally and very importantly, it must be taken as a decisive episode in the political history of modern France.

In their accounts of the Dreyfus Affair historians have differed over the extent to which one or more of these aspects should be stressed. Additional disagreement is found not only among the conclusions reached but also over the very method of approach.

Until the past decade or two many who wrote about the Affair had participated in it, or were old enough to have been profoundly affected by the events which took place. While not necessarily rendered less useful, their histories often reflect the role played or the position taken at the time. As a socialist deputy, Alexandre Zévaès became an ardent Dreyfusard and his account deals harshly with the General Staff, the Church, and other forces seen as reactionary and creating obstacles in the pursuit of truth and justice. Joseph Reinach was a leading revisionist and prominent in having the Dreyfus case reopened; his rich and authoritative seven volume history, still a basic source, presents the accepted revisionist interpretation. Henri Dutrait-Crozon, on the other hand, approved the raising of the national interest as the supreme consideration and thus assumed that any diminution of that interest, particularly on behalf of a Jewish officer convicted of treason, necessarily originated in the work of a powerful and traitorous organization, one with resources great enough to bribe the corrupt Esterhazy to confess to a crime he did not commit.

This presentation of early Dreyfusard and anti-Dreyfusard views is headed by the penetrating account of Nicholas Halasz, which stresses the hysterical fervor that swept over the nation and disrupted and transformed all aspects of daily life. The section is concluded by the testimony of

vii

the German military attaché, Colonel von Schwartzkoppen; it displays the German side of the Affair and, in charging Esterhazy with the crime of which Dreyfus was accused, is conformable to revisionist thinking.

The organization of the remainder of this volume has been determined largely by the issues necessarily dealt with by later historians of the Affair. All of them must reply somehow to questions like the following: Was the General Staff good or bad, wise or foolish in its actions? How much importance should be attached to anti-semitism as providing both the background of the Affair and the context within which it developed? Was there a plot on the part of conservatives and nationalists to bring down the republic regarded as hostile to French political and religious traditions? Who was actually guilty of spying for Germany, and why was he guilty of it? Given the enormous impact made by the Affair both on contemporaries and on those to win power in the future, what were its consequences for French history? For Western Civilization?

Accordingly, excerpts from histories of the Dreyfus Affair have been divided into three groups. The first presents the conflicting opinions expressed about its origins and reveals that the arguments used originally by the people involved in the Affair are by no means outdated. Some historians, like most of the revisionists, have insisted on the presence of a reactionary, clerico-military plot to overthrow the existing Republic. One such writer is Jacques Kayser, and like Zévaès, he also stresses the role of anti-semitism as making intelligible the early assumption of guilt on the part of Dreyfus' superiors. Jacques Bainville, on the other hand, presents what might be called the classical conservative interpretation. It upholds the sincerity of the General Staff, finds Dreyfus guilty — thus invalidating any confession made by Esterhazy, and regrets the growth of "radicalism" in the wake of the Affair.

The second group contains the most recent historical contributions to an understanding of the Dreyfus Affair. François Goguel has thickened the mystery of the identity of the spy or spies by adducing the existence of two guilty parties. Within the past few years, writers like the Englishman, Guy Chapman, and the Frenchman, Marcel Thomas, have preferred to de-emphasize the personal guilt or innocence of the leading characters and to examine instead what might be called the mechanics of the Affair. That is, they discuss and evaluate the Army, Church, and Parliament as institutions and the activities of the protagonists chiefly within this framework. Chapman in particular rejects unconditionally the conspiracy thesis and deflates enormously the influence of anti-semitism; for him the Dreyfus Affair was the result of a legitimate error committed by the General Staff, and the Case is thus relegated to causes wholly accidental. Finally, in the last grouping, we see how the writers described and commented on either what they viewed as the larger context within which the Affair developed, or its political and social consequences.

The Dreyfus Case would stand out in French history if only for the spate of anti-clerical legislation which emanated from it. Disappointed anti-revisionists saw the suppression of religious orders, the separation of church and state, and the furthering of state control over education as a "Dreyfusian revolution." Jacques Chastenet criticizes the vindictive, if triumphant, Dreyfusards and sees their plan to take revenge on the Army as a threat to national security. He admires the foresight of those who managed to substitute the Church as a target and thus preserved the ability of France to defend herself. Dreyfusards, however, holding clerical influence responsible for the condemnation of the Jewish officer and seeing in it a cause of France's difficulties, eagerly took steps to disarm the Church and republicanize the Army. This story is told in the analyses of François Goguel and Roger Soltau, both of whom are concerned here with the larger issues of the Dreyfus

Affair. While insisting that the Affair only strengthened political alignments already in existence, Rudolph Winnacker describes the coming of the revisionists to power as bringing a "new deal" to French politics. Looking into the future, Wilhelm Herzog ends his book on the Dreyfus Affair with the Pétain Affair and describes the Vichy regime as the belated revenge of anti-Dreyfusard generals.

On a broader canvas there is the conclusion, admittedly pessimistic, of Hannah Arendt, who saw the vast concern with justice for an individual as belonging only to the nineteenth century, to the dying world of the rights of man. She denotes the mob action, the anti-semitic leagues, and the attempted *coups* as portents of the twentieth century totalitarianism struggling to be born. (It was a similar interpretation of the Dreyfus Affair that led Theodore Herzl to become interested in the fate of his co-religionists and to conclude that if one of the most civilized countries in Europe could permit such intolerance, then Jews could expect no safety except in a national state of their own.)

The conflict which lay at the heart of the Affair, that between the demands of national security and the affirmation of individual rights, supplies its greatest lesson. For a period of time what most Frenchmen considered the national interest took precedence over every other concern, including that for individual justice. The experience is not without parallel in our own day, where even among those devoted to securing human freedom, some have been persuaded by the threat of foreign aggression to deny, in its name, the exercize of certain basic rights.

But the Dreyfus Affair also demonstrated how a relatively small group striving to ensure justice for one individual triumphed over a majority convinced of the need to repress it. The heroic aspect of the Case should not be slighted. Despite the opportunism which may have led revisionists to take political advantage of their newly-found popularity, the Affair remains the prime example of a few men who gathered enough courage to withstand hostile public opinion and thus helped to preserve the institutions that could enable others to do the same. Jean Jaurès, one of the more important Dreyfusards, paid the greatest tribute when he said of them, "What matter the errors of fate and false directions of life? A few luminous and fervent hours are enough to give meaning to a lifetime."

The Conflict of Opinion

"A reactionary nationalist movement was taking shape, directed both against the foreigner, and especially against Germany, and inwards against the Jew, represented as a profiteer and agent of the foreigner, and the socialist, as the creator of disorder."

— Jacques Kayser

"To accept the conventional reading of a clerico-military conspiracy is to swallow the propaganda of the Dreyfusards. No conspiracy existed in military circles, none in clerical. . . . And . . . anti-semitism throughout was no more than an accessory."

— Guy Chapman

"We have only sought, on our part, to understand and make understood the internal mechanism of a judicial episode the complexity of which was derived above all from its collective and administrative character. The drama of the individual crushed — without understanding why or how — by the indifferent wheels of a well-oiled machine that must be destroyed in order to be stopped, is doubtless not without relevance."

— Marcel Thomas

"The *bordereau* was the work not of Dreyfus but of Esterhazy. Therein lies the fact which excludes the guilt of Dreyfus . . ."

— Alexandre Zévaès

"The Court passed by the decisive objections raised by Esterhazy's confession, ignored the fact that he had modelled his handwriting on a poor facsimile of the *bordereau* given to him . . . The Court left this point in the shadows not even wishing to direct public attention to the thesis of 'Esterhazy, straw-man of the Jews,' which is the key to the Dreyfus Affair."

— Henri Dutrait-Crozon

"It is difficult to believe that [Esterhazy] was guilty of all the deeds of which Dreyfus was accused. This was the primary argument of the anti-revisionists and it was never completely refuted. . . . This is why, to take into account the amazing complexities of the Affair, it is necessary in my opinion, to suppose the existence of two guilty parties."

— François Goguel

". . . the Dreyfus Affair ruined the government of moderates and the Conservative Republic. . . . It produced the coming of this 'radicalism' which the wisest republicans had feared and contained. Within the Republic it led to a revolution which threatened to dissolve everything. The war was approached in a state of complete dissolution."

— Jacques Bainville

"The Dreyfus Affair merely speeded up a movement in French politics which had been gathering force since the beginning of the last decade of the nineteenth century."

— RUDOLPH A. WINNACKER

"The Army and the principal economic enterprises were to be saved only by the sacrifice of the religious congregations and the certified church."

— JACQUES CHASTENET

"The Dreyfus Case, complex as it was, can be reduced ultimately to a simple choice between two conceptions of society which had, ever since the Revolution, been struggling for mastery in the French mind . . . the basing of society and civilization on certain elementary individual rights, the other based on authority as external and prior to individual citizens."

— ROGER SOLTAU

"Not the Dreyfus Case with its trials but the Dreyfus Affair in its entirety offers a foregleam of the twentieth century."

— HANNAH ARENDT

I. THE IMPASSIONED AFFAIR:
DREYFUSARDS *versus* ANTI-DREYFUSARDS

The Story of a Mass Hysteria

NICHOLAS HALASZ

The author of this recent best-seller about the Dreyfus Affair lived in France, but since 1941 has made his home in the United States. He has written extensively in European periodicals on law, philosophy, social psychology, and history, and has acted as foreign correspondent for European, Canadian, and American newspapers. His account describes the disorder and passion in the struggle between Dreyfusards and anti-Dreyfusards, and thus offers an explanation for the length of the Affair and for the bitterness it was to leave behind.

So began a morality play that was to achieve a grandeur unparalleled in the history of the modern state and make France examine in fire and in fear the bedrock upon which democracy is founded. The sanctity of the individual, yes. A noble ideal, no doubt. But as a practical matter, should the whole be sacrificed for the minutest part? Is the moral vindication of one Frenchman worth jeopardizing the security of all Frenchmen?

In facing the question, France, the nation of reason, went out of her mind. Normal life stopped. Only a handful of men retained faith in the ability of democracy to provide security for all. The rest had faith only in the State and its Army, and went into paroxysms over any act that reflected on it. In the words of a contemporary writer, "Heroism was needed even to utter the word 'justice.' To protest against the violation of right was made out a crime, and to doubt the infallibility of a military court was considered treason."

Governments fell. Eventually no court, not even the highest, was trusted. The Chamber of Deputies passed a law to prevent France's highest criminal court from considering the matter further. With courts unable to rule in law, the nation came to the brink of anarchy. The fact that the truth was discovered very soon after the nation had accepted the lie made no difference. The lie had to continue to be accepted. To reject it was to reject the material force of the Army as a shield against Germany and embrace instead an abstract ideal as a refuge from brutal violence. The nation refused to do it. It sided with the lie and declared it the only truth. . . .

But the climate was worsening. It was no longer enough merely not to impeach the General Staff. One had to beat one's breast in favor of it. The Minister of Labor paused in the Chamber for a moment's chat with Scheurer. So great was the muttering that he hastened to take the floor to announce that he had only asked his col-

1

league for the address of a pastry shop. President Faure had had the bad luck to receive Scheurer as a visitor on some legislative matter. He asked Scheurer to deny that they had spoken about the Dreyfus case. General Billot issued a statement that the latest events had not shaken the Government's view that the case was closed. The statement seemed too temperate to the press. A storm of abuse was unleashed. The War Minister was accused of allowing his personal debts to be paid by Scheurer and Joseph Reinach. He was "exposed" as having stolen 100,000 francs from the Army's secret fund, and was declared to be selling out the Army of which he was guardian to the "Jewish syndicate." *La Libre Parole* published a sensational article accusing the President and the Cabinet of being Dreyfus' accomplices in espionage.

The Catholic youth held a protest meeting and adopted resolutions: no one should deprive France's soldiers of the confidence they had in their leaders; Jews should be excluded from the Army and from the civil service. Posters went up all over Paris with a message from the Royal Pretender, Philippe d'Orléans. Conscious of his duty, his rights and the virtue of monarchical institutions, the unemployed heir to a nonexistent throne assured the nation of his capacity to defend the honor of French soldiers. Royalist-minded students blocked traffic for a riotous demonstration in front of *Le Figaro*.

Day by day the press rehashed "proofs" of a world-wide conspiracy whose aim was to destroy the Army and thus France. One of the greatest orators of the day, the Catholic Albert de Mun, took the floor of the Chamber of Deputies to interpolate in the proceedings a few remarks:

We must reveal the facts about the mysterious and occult power, strong enough to throw suspicion on the commanders of the Army, on the men who have to lead the Army and direct the war when the hour strikes. Let us discover whether that power is great enough to subvert the entire country. . . . You wonder perhaps whether my interpolation is not inspired by party considerations. No, we know no government and opposition. There are here today only . . . Frenchmen anxious to preserve that common domain of our unflagging hopes — the honor of the Army.

The Chamber rushed through a resolution paying homage to the Army and excoriating those who instigated odious campaigns to disturb public confidence.

It seemed almost as if Esterhazy, who had wanted only a little corner on the General Staff from which he might empty wastebaskets and peer into files, was going to end up as Minister of War, firing the generals who had refused to hire him. The press, including not only the anti-Semitic sheets but *Le Matin* and *Le Petit Journal*, discovered that the "Jewish syndicate" it had invented had its headquarters in Berlin, that it had spent 6,000,000 francs already in forging documents and corrupting prominent Frenchmen, and that for two years now the French Government had been in possession of the names of those acting as the syndicate's chiefs. . . .

Maurice Barrès, novelist and Boulangist deputy, developed the astonishing creed of the new nationalism. He initiated the cult of the graveyards. The French, he wrote, have accepted as their guide the pillar of light in the sky, forgetting that the real light is under their feet and in the tombs of their ancestors. Their only salvation is to prostrate themselves before their dead and their soil, and, in the spirit of penitents, to take these unto themselves. Even atheists ought to be Catholics, added Jules Soury, another theoretician of this school, not for the sake of the Catholic faith, but in order to live like their ancestors who had been believers and to meditate on the same maxims of life.

In the eyes of the nationalists, the Protestants stood outside of the nation. To be faithful to France in the mere world of intellect was not enough. The Protestants, unlike the Catholics, could never be part of that physico-mental continuum which mystically encompassed the nation.

To the Church militant the time seemed

to have arrived. The nation, as if by a miracle, was ready to come back under the wings of the Church. The Pope had advised the French Church to recognize the lay Republic as having been permitted by God. This was construed as constituting a misreading of French history. The throne might never be restored, but it was believed that France could be turned into a Catholic state. A hundred years of history were being reversed. The nation was returning as an errant sheep to the fold.

The new, reactionary nationalism fed on the frustrated greatness of a people torn between the fear of a new invasion and the passion to prevail over such an invasion — a passion expressed in *revanche*. The Army was their shield in all trials.

And yet, in the case of one Jewish captain found to have been a traitor by seven of his fellow officers, a stubborn clique insisted on incriminating the military court and the General Staff rather than the convicted Jew. The papers which the public read, the men whose opinions it respected, asserted that the clique consisted of Protestants and a few intellectuals, misguidedly invoking the principles of the Revolution. The public also read and heard that in the Protestant countries and in countries where the influence of Jews and Free Masons prevailed, public opinion unanimously demanded that France destroy her Army rather than keep a Jew deported — all in the name of the principles of the Revolution. The fear grew that the nation might become the victim of her own principles. Would it not be better to sacrifice the principles and settle for survival? A consistent, purposeful, and determined coalition of institutions, church and royalist, right and center, vested with the prestige of a long tradition and endowed with all the means for shaping public opinion, put the choice on this basis: the Revolution's Rights of Man must die, or France must.

To the majority of the people, the Revolution still meant the end of the feudal system of privileges, the advent of national unity and the triumph of the sovereignty of the people. And the majority of the people kept voting for the republican parties, solidly and increasingly. But on the unique issue of the Army, where the security of the nation, so they believed, was at stake, they were ready to follow the Church militant, the authoritarians, the anti-Semites and the royalists, and even sacrifice the Republic itself rather than face the fact that the Army which they regarded as their only salvation was untrustworthy. . . .

La Croix and other newspapers of the Assumptionist Order followed suit, heralding the crusade against the enemies of the Army and of Christ. And parish priests of five thousand churches throughout France echoed the battle cry.

The aristocracy descended into the political arena. People who had kept aloof in their castles or secluded in their salons responded to the call. Their young joined the mobs on the streets. Adults went to mass meetings, mixing freely with anarchists, Drumont's anti-Semites and Déroulède's patriots, in a combined effort to destroy the bourgeois republic.

Esterhazy's acquittal created a morally upside-down world. In the words of the young journalist Paul Brulat, "the fraudulent glorified fraud, and the impostors erected a monument to imposture." The public sang hosannas to a criminal whose crime was being expiated by another man.

Such moral enormity could be sustained only in an atmosphere of terror and intolerance. It was the popular press that silenced dissent. It went after people, demolished their position in life, material or moral, and exposed them to contempt. In their fear of the invented "syndicate" the people had created a real power of destruction. A teacher in Paris told Clemenceau: Do not expect high-school teachers to come out for you. If I gave you my name, I would soon find myself retired, to rot somewhere in the depths of Brittany.

The terror did not come from the Government. The Government itself was terrorized. So were the deputies in the Chamber. The nationalists and clericals by themselves could not have silenced dissent by sheer threat. It was the people. The bulk of the nation had identified itself with the Army. Yet even with the Army secure from Dreyfus, the feeling of insecurity continued. The offensive continued — but where was the enemy? And where was the opposition? When Paul Brulat was asked by a foreigner, "Where are the honest men in this country?" he replied, "They are frightened." No tyranny weighs heavier on society, Brulat added, than the tyranny of public opinion. It crucified Jesus, burned John Hus and Savonarola at the stake, it persecuted Galileo, delivered apostles and martyrs to the hangman. . . .

But in her domestic ordeal France resented the interference even of such friendly nations as Russia. Following Zola's protest, the internal tensions broke into violence. In Nantes, Bordeaux, Toulouse, Montpellier, Le Havre, and Orléans huge crowds plundered Jewish stores, beat up Jews, publicly burned Zola's article and hung Zola in effigy. In Paris the mob paraded along the boulevards carrying standards: "Death to Zola! Death to the Jews!" Huge protest meetings were held, ending in bloody clashes. For a month or more, the towns all over the country were in an uproar. The police were often powerless to prevent bloodshed, and the military had to be called out. In Algiers, pogroms claimed numerous victims, French and Arabs making common cause in raiding Jewish shops.

In Paris, the police were called to keep students from storming Zola's house. The students had to content themselves with stoning it and shouting, "Death to Zola! Long live the Army!" At universities in Belgium, Italy, and Switzerland resolutions were passed hailing Zola's stand for justice. In France only the few who had privately dissented all along dared to raise their voices. Many French intellectuals inscribed their names on a list to do homage to Zola.

The country was possessed of violent excitement. No time, thought, or passion seemed left for the business of everyday life. Life consisted of turning to the papers, arming oneself with arguments, fighting with the word and the fist. People ceased to read books or to go to the theater. No thriller, no play could compete with the drama of which France was the stage, her citizens the actors, and the civilized world the audience.

This fever was destined to keep a hold of varying intensity on the country for years. The constant awareness of conflicting and contradictory events vested life with the magic of a higher plane of existence. The man in the street re-evaluated the past, revised principles, and spoke his mind. Life was lived as if every day were a red-letter one, towering over that gray maze of time which, in the ordinary run, is wasted on petty, individual cares. . . .

In the tidal wave of anti-Semitism that swept over the country, many towns organized boycotts on Jewish shops. Petitions to expel from France the Jews and all those who defended them rained down on the Government. Laws were demanded to deprive the Jews of the vote. The nationalist press incited employers to dismiss Jewish workers. In Algiers, popular meetings and the press urged that Jewish children be excluded from schools, Jewish employees thrown out of the civil service. Even the medieval charge of ritual murder was rehashed.

The Catholic press went straight to the heart of the matter. The Great Revolution was described as an insurrection of man against God and was called the original sin of the century. Gleefully it rejected the Rights of Man and mounted an offensive on intellectual freedom. At a college festival presided over by a general, a Catholic priest pleaded for authority through power:

When I speak of the necessity for a nation to arm itself with power I mean the material power that does not reason, but imposes itself — the power of which the Army is the most forceful expression, the power of the cannon, which is the ultimate argument of statesmen and of nations. . . . The enemy is intellectualism which professes to disdain power. Turn the point of the sword against it. Woe to the government that veils its weakness behind a supposed insufficiency of legal powers and lets the sword drop. The country in the grip of anxiety will reject those who refuse to save her even at the price of bloodshed.

A poet, asked to write a poem to celebrate in the Pantheon the centenary of the historian Michelet, was made to strike out the lines in which his poem appealed to France to show the world that she still was the champion of right and justice.

The left-wing intellectuals sounded the tocsin for battle. They revived the Society of the Rights of the Man and of the Citizen. On the Right, Paul Déroulède resuscitated his League of Patriots, dissolved when Boulangism ebbed. . . .

Royalists, Catholics, and authoritarians began preparing for a civil war. By this action of the Right, the strange phenomenon of the "Dreyfusian revolution" was set in motion. For that is the accepted name of the unrest which from 1898 onward almost brought to a standstill the pursuits of public and private life in France, substituting for them meetings, demonstrations, brawls, debates, the organizing of *coups d'état* and of forces to forestall them. Families and friendships broke up forever, new human relations formed.

Léon Blum in his reminiscences compared these times to the Great Revolution: the individual's life ceased to matter. He was ready to be sacrificed without hesitation for the cause of truth and justice, nor would he have hesitated to sacrifice the lives of his opponents. And his adversaries in their turn burned with equal eagerness to defend what they considered the nation's vital interests, no matter who died.

People of all persuasions were out "to look beyond the pursuits of life towards the Ideals, or towards the Chimaera — but to something that transcended their own daily interests," as a contemporary English periodical put it.

Curiously, it was a happy life, not only because it became elevated and meaningful, but because one lived with and among friends who held the same opinion on the case. Family ties were not strong enough to stand the strain of diverging opinions, and agreement made intimate friends of people who otherwise fitted ill together. Elegant aristocrats hailed the butcher boys of the Anti-Semitic League at mass meetings and conservative academicians shared the platform with revolutionary syndicalists. Melchior de Vogüé's words may be accepted as true: "Above shrewd interests and criminal passions, the bravest hearts of France rushed upon each other in the dark with equal nobility of sentiment, exasperated by the awesome conflict. . . ."

Lectures at the universities became a problem. They were interrupted by demonstrations by the members of the Anti-Semite Youth; or of the Committee of Royalist Youth; or by Jules Guérin's anti-Semitic shock troops; or else by the Socialist Youth. The demonstrations usually ended up in street fights.

The revisionist youth set up headquarters in a bookshop run by the poet Charles Péguy on the Rue de Cujas in the Latin Quarter. Serious young men gathered there who wished to broaden the fight for justice in the Dreyfus case into a fight for justice to all. Christians, or humanitarians, they eventually became Socialists, followers of Jaurès, who, as they earnestly hoped, would lead them, not into class struggles but toward social reform based on a moral renascence. Some began by fighting the depraved General Staff only to become anti-militarists or pacifists.

The Dreyfus Affair was omnipresent. In the theater Ibsen's *An Enemy of the People* caused a free-for-all. One sentence sounded as if it were an allusion to Zola. The play was withdrawn. Jules Renard in his diary mentions a young man whose family desired him to marry a certain young girl. He requested her parents to let him have her photograph and also to inform him of her views on the Dreyfus

Affair. A French expedition to the Arctic wintered on an iceberg and was feared lost. In the spring they were found safe and sound. Their first question to the rescuers was "What about Dreyfus? Is he free?"

Scores of duels were fought between former friends on account of the affair. The publisher Stock mentions thirty in the circle of his acquaintance. A number of suicides were committed in this context, not without suspicion of murder arising on one side or the other.

The battle was carried on in hundreds of pamphlets. It seemed that almost everybody wished to make a public declaration of his stand. There were devastating cartoons. The greatest hit was scored by a picture in two sections. The first showed a large and happy family gathering around a richly laden table. The caption read: "They have not yet spoken of *it*." The second showed the same place turned upside down in fiendish disorder, everyone gesticulating, hurling insults. The caption read: "They spoke of *it*." . . .

Paris in those days was in the throes of constructing a subway. The *Métro* was to be completed for the World Exhibition of 1900. The workers involved in the construction went on strike. The Government called out the Army, in fear of sabotage and disturbances. The streets took on the look of encampments. Wild rumors of a revolution appeared in the papers abroad. In France, inspired reports flew about: conspiracy between the striking workers and the Dreyfusards; general plans for a *coup d'état*; Dreyfus back, held at Mont Valérien; Dreyfus dead; Esterhazy hanged. The reports were printed in the nationalist press. *L'Aurore* presented its readers with the version that Henry had not committed suicide; the Jesuits, the paper said, had put a razor in his hand. He had been forced to choose: degradation and deportation or else suicide with a pension for his widow and the Dreyfus revision buried.

Truth had a thorny path to travel. And the end was still years away.

The Hostility of the General Staff

ALEXANDRE ZÉVAÈS

At the time of the Dreyfus Affair, Zévaès was a socialist deputy, first a Marxist inspired by Jules Guesde, then an independent social democrat. He has written extensively on the Third Republic, both histories and biographies. His impassioned account of the Affair, although appearing many years later, shows how strongly he was affected by it, and his reactions were those of the Dreyfusards. In these pages, taken from the chapter entitled, "The Political Situation of the Army in 1894," he emphasized the anti-semitism of the General Staff.

An officer in the French Army, a captain of artillery, certified by the General Staff, accused of treason, condemned by a court-martial to perpetual deportation, degraded in the presence of troops and in the midst of the booing and howling of a maddened crowd, despatched to the most distant and savage island, returned to France in a special cruiser by virtue of a decree issued by the supreme court annulling the court-martial's decision, prosecuted a second time under military jurisdiction and a second time found guilty by it, pardoned the day after his condemnation, proclaimed innocent by the supreme court, the object of a new request for revision, reintegrated into the Army with the rank of major by issue of a special law, finally decorated with the Legion of Honor in the court of the military school in which he had been subjected to the punishment of degradation; what dramatist has ever conceived of a story as tragic, as poignant, as stupendous?

The condemnation, which will be shown as illegal and unjust, the atrocious torture, the flesh martyrized at Devil's Island, and the solemn rehabilitation that followed, all constitute, however, only one of the elements of the drama which History calls the Dreyfus Affair.

The Dreyfus Affair, as a matter of fact, is not only one but several cases; it is the entire nation aroused, gripped by passion and fever, panting and in agony, taking part in a drama of heroic grandeur, in which two tragic choruses attacked each other, successively coming to power on the stage called France and in the theatre of the world.

The Dreyfus Affair is political and social life upset from top to bottom; it is parties tossed about by events and deeply divided, even families disunited, the oldest friendships broken, people arguing with and cursing each other in meetings, on trolley platforms, in cafés, theatres, clubs, in alleys, and at tables.

Within the chambers and before their tribunes there are repeated interpellations, motions to present government and private bills, of which the case of the condemned captain is the object for three years.

There are demonstrations overflowing from the vast meeting halls onto the public squares, attempts to create civil war by the nationalist parties, plots and experiments with military *coups d'état*; rumors of violence are answered by the rattling of swords; anti-Dreyfusards take the street by assault, they are then conquered by Drey

From Alexandre Zévaès, *L'Affaire Dreyfus* (Paris: Éditions de la Nouvelle Revue Critique, 1931), pp. 7–14, 19–21, 30–32, 210. Translated by the editor.

fusards and remain definitely in possession of the latter.

The Dreyfus Affair, in short, is a political crisis as serious, but socially more profound, than those of the Moral Order and Boulangism, in which the republican regime is successfully defended.

But how has the condemnation of an innocent man been possible? How and why, when the proofs of his innocence become more resounding each day, can an entire party persist in raising obstacles to the reopening of his trial?

These questions will not be answered if it is not recalled what was, in November, 1894 — that is, at the moment of the arrest of Captain Alfred Dreyfus — the political situation in France, and what was, at that time, the attitude characteristic of the Army.

Casimir-Périer was then President of the Republic, elected June 27, 1894, to replace Sadi Carnot. Charles Dupuy, since June 1, was President of the Council of Ministers. The Republic appeared in a state of lethargy, immobile and languishing. It appeared exhausted by the effort required, five years earlier, to break the ceasarian *coup* of a seditious general.

Anarchist attacks, dynamite explosions, and Caserio's dagger-thrust had furnished the pretext for the laws of December 12, 1893, and July 28, 1894, restricting the freedom of the press.

The legislative elections of August 20, 1894, had attested to the growth of socialism, and now, with Jules Guesde, Jean Jaurès, and Édouard Vaillant as its chief spokesmen, the movement saw raised against it an ever tighter coalition of the center and the right.

The Opportunists of yesterday, Gambetta, Jules Ferry, and Paul Bert, had been replaced by the Progressists — a new team of ministers and ministerial candidates — whose chiefs included Barthou, Burdeau, Charles Dupuy, Deschanel, and Poincaré; men unable to justify their readiness for advancement with any boldness of thought or spirit of reform.

Wearied of continually sterile and useless opposition, yesterday's Monarchists had become *ralliés*, and accommodating themselves to the Republic tried to introduce a conservative spirit within it. The most ardent, most violent groupings on the right now referred to themselves as antisemites and nationalists.

Anti-semitism, whose mask of anti-financierism testified to the existence of a credulous element of public opinion, claimed France for the French and declared war on the Jews: and not only on the Jews but on those not opposed to Jews. Step-by-step it fought Protestants, free-masons, free-thinkers, all those who did not incline themselves before the domination of the Church. In short, it was the spirit of free enquiry itself which was denounced by anti-semitism.

In France the promoter of anti-semitism was Édouard Drumont. His two volumes of *La France Juive* had appeared in 1886 and summed up his program. *La Libre Parole,* founded in 1892, was the movement's newspaper.

Nationalism, a new word popularized by Maurice Barrès, exploited the idea of the country. It made appeals to chauvinism, exalted the sword, and sought the triumph of a military dictatorship.

These nationalist and anti-semitic tendencies were particularly popular among Army officers, above all, among higher ranking officers.

The new "social order," of which Gambetta, in his resounding Grenoble speech, had prophesied the coming, and which before him, in terms equally strong, had been announced by such men as Chateaubriand, Royer-Collard, Tocqueville, and Prévost-Paradol; this "new order" was only the Third Estate, the democratic and laboring *petite-bourgeoisie,* and members of it had managed to enter the chambers and government by means of universal suffrage. They were upstarts in the highest positions of the civil service and government; it was seen that the son of a modest grocer of Cahors had become President of the Council. But the Army and Navy had resisted this incursion. The students of the rue des Postes had jealously retained the highest ranks for themselves. Reactionaries and clerics, however, feared that neither the Army nor the Navy would escape their influence or their leadership much longer.

The Army had seen itself invaded by the sons of artisans and peasants who had won scholarships, passed through the *lycée*, and who, occasionally, by work and talent, had won braid. And plebeians, freethinkers, and Israelites not only entered and contaminated the Army, but even succeeded in placing themselves on the General Staff. What did they plan to do, these republicans whose beliefs contradicted the principle of passive obedience and were incompatible with caesarian militarism? Above all, what did those Jews plan to do, who, having renounced the commercial and financial dealings found appropriate by their coreligionists, proposed to follow a military career? What evil thoughts of gain attracted them here? Or what treason did they think of carrying out? The time had come to chase them away.

At the time of the examinations for the School of War, General Bonnefond had awarded to two Israelite officers of the line grades entirely lower than deserved, avowing to his surprised colleagues "that it is not necessary to have Jews on the General Staff." And he added, "You know the source of our intelligence about foreign armies, and that Italian Jews, German Jews, and Romanian Jews sell us whatever information we want about their respective countries. And you would like to install Jews on our General Staff! Why would the French Jew be any different? That is why I failed those gentlemen." Such was the prevailing state of mind in high military spheres.

The Minister of War in the Dupuy Cabinet was General Mercier. Conceited, boastful of his "artilleryman's nose," he was not devoid of knowledge, and, endowed with that bombastic eloquence which easily arouses applause, was a good speaker. . . .

At the head of the General Staff, where he had replaced General de Mirabel — who had already staffed it with his creatures — was General Le Mouton de Boisdeffre, who, like his principal collaborator, General Gonse, placed his conscience in the keeping of R. P. Dulac, of the Company of Jesus, with whom he had a daily conference.

The Intelligence Service, in which, under its title of the "Statistical Section," were gathered the forces of espionage and counter-espionage, had as chief, Colonel Sandherr. A former Protestant converted to Catholicism, a violent anti-semite who publicly affirmed that all Jews were scoundrels, he was already suffering from the creeping paralysis which forced his retirement in 1895 and carried him away in 1897.

Under Colonel Sandherr's orders worked Major Henry, also anti-semitic, correspondent for *La Libre Parole*, taken from the ranks, but poorly educated and with limited intelligence.

At still the same office was Major du Paty de Clam, again an anti-semite, who had passionately taken up spiritualism, who saw spies everywhere, and who for two years had one of his cousins followed under the pretext that the latter spoke several languages and travelled extensively.

From the Minister to the commoner Henry, and especially among the higher officers, all were afflicted with the most stubborn caste spirit.

It was these men who put the Dreyfus Affair into operation. . . .

The *bordereau* was thus on the point of being filed when, on October 6, it was given to Lt. Colonel d'Aboville, deputy-chief of the 4th Bureau, just returned from leave. He proceeded by reason. It appeared evident that first, the author of the *bordereau* was an artillery officer. It was no less evident that the officer had been involved with the 3rd Bureau, because he possessed the new artillery manual, with the 2nd

Bureau, because he was concerned with new field formations, with the 2nd or 3rd Bureaus because he knew about the Madagascar expedition, and with the 3rd Bureau since he spoke of "supporting troops" and even specified that the new plan would modify their movements. The circle of inquiry was therefore singularly limited and only a probationer — d'Aboville insisted on this point — was in a position to supply the documents enumerated in the *bordereau* because, under orders not to discuss their work, officers attached to the various departments of the General Staff were seldom in touch, while probationers alone passed successively through all of them.

That established, d'Aboville consulted the list of probationers. His anti-semitism made him stop at once at the name of Dreyfus. Of course! The traitor could only be a Jew. He compared the writing of Dreyfus with that of the *bordereau*. There was no longer any doubt. He had discovered the culprit.

Colonel Fabré eagerly associated himself with the discovery. Both immediately informed Gonse, Boisdeffre, and Sandherr. The last struck his forehead and cried, "A Jew! I should have suspected it."

Supplementary verifications, very simple ones, moreover, should have been made. The author of the *bordereau* had told his correspondent that he was "going on manoeuvres." It would have been easy to learn whether Dreyfus had gone on manoeuvres. He had not. Furthermore, (and this ruins all the hypotheses of Lt. Colonel d'Aboville), within the small circle of probationary officers where he placed the culprit, none had taken part in manoeuvres.

And then, was the author necessarily an artillery officer? There is no doubt that two of the notes delivered and those offered for delivery were concerned with the artillery. But the terms used were inaccurate and would not have come from anyone with technical training. He would not write "120" for "120 limited," "hydraulic brake" for "hydropneumatic brake," "way in which that part is conducted" in place

of "way in which it behaves." . . . But d'Aboville, Fabré, and Sandherr were too proud, too happy with their discovery to pause at such trifles. . . .

At last, on November 1, *La Libre Parole* ran a headline in enormous letters: "High Treason; Arrest of the Jewish Officer, Alfred Dreyfus." Then every other newspaper reported the story.

On November 3 General Saussier, military-governor of Paris, signed the order of inquiry. The investigation was confided to Major d'Ormescheville.

The anti-semitic and clerical press at once broke loose with great violence. Did not the deed justify all the previous campaigns against the presence of Israelites in the Army? "The Tsar knows what he is doing when he excludes them from his army, from his empire," cried *Le Pélegrin*. "It is the Jewish enemy betraying France," confirmed *La Croix*. "The Jew is only a mixture of thief, ruffian, and swine," proclaimed *Le Triboulet*. *La Libre Parole,* by way of suggesting future investigations, published lists of Israelite officers in both the Army and Navy. . . .

General Mercier, far from taking alarm at the excitement of the press and trying to restrain it, sought to re-enforce the violence at the same time that he was instructing members of the court-martial how to vote. On two occasions, in two interviews, given to *Le Matin* (November 17) and to *Le Figaro* (November 27), he declared that the guilt of Dreyfus was indisputable.

The President of the Council, Charles Dupuy, showed himself no less prudent. On Monday, December 10, he told an audience that until then he had not "taken seriously that which it was convenient to call Jewish power," but he now understood that it constituted "an alarming fact that the Government will soon have to face with cold blood." He added, without laughing, "that someone dared to offer a million to the court-martial's reporting officer if the latter consented, not to recommend a verdict of innocent, but merely to voice doubts as to guilt."

While the President of the Council so expressed himself, while the Minister of War affirmed in advance the guilt of the accused, what independence, what freedom of mind was left to officers summoned by this Ministry to constitute a court-martial which already understood only orders, discipline, and hierarchy? Now it was under these conditions that Alfred Dreyfus was deferred to it. . . .

If the Affair developed into a question of race, religion, and regime, it was due to the anti-semitism and clericalism of those who opposed revision and who worked to make of it an issue for or against Jews in the Army. Even after Henry's suicide they persisted and included as objects of attack free-thinkers and Protestants. Thus the entire cause of religious toleration was involved. Because clerical generals wished to keep an innocent man in penal servitude and retain command of the Army for Jesuit students, they did not hesitate to raise themselves arrogantly against the civil power of France, against the republican regime, and to threaten a French jury with their collective resignation.

Esterhazy the Culprit

JOSEPH REINACH

The first significant account of the Dreyfus Affair, still the most complete and the one taken as a point of departure by present-day historians, is the seven-volume history of Joseph Reinach. Although for many years a Moderate in the Chamber of Deputies and bitterly opposed to socialism, Reinach, as one of the first Dreyfusards, worked long and hard for revision and, in the capacity of friend and adviser to Waldeck-Rousseau, suggested that a socialist be included in the latter's Ministry of Republican Defense, formed in 1899 to bring an end to the Affair. The volumes comprising his history are well-documented but, as we shall see, several of his interpretations and in particular his theory about the arrival of the *bordereau*, have been questioned.

THUS, by September, 1894, it was hardly a year that Mercier had been Minister and his star was fading so quickly that people forgot it had ever sparkled. He was the object of almost general misgivings, mingled with disappointment. Casimir-Périer, who had advanced his career, regretted having launched such a blunderer. Mercier's principal colleagues studied his enigmatic features with anxiety. He had disagreed with, one after the other, the diverse factions in the Chamber, and was becoming suspect to anyone familiar with military affairs. The demogogic or revolutionary press was no longer alone in attacking him, but had been joined by the entire political press, regardless of party affiliation, and except for official newspapers, by the military press as well. Public opinion, in turn bewildered and wearied by his lack of method, his insolent frivolity, and his guise of a comedian in search of applause, wondered whether he was not a public danger. Finally, in the Army, from the ordinary soldier shaken by contradictory orders, to the highest officers irritated with his vanity and disdain, and feeling the controls of the vast machine slipping between his imprudent hands, a cry was raised against him, against the most tiresome minister to be called in many years to the War Department. There he was viewed as a politician without conscience and a creator of disorder.

Other ministers of war had been attacked in the past, often violently, but for their attitude and political ambitions; he was first denounced for incapacity. His befuddled and presumptuous incompetence became legendary. Only the men of his profession knew the seriousness of some of his shortcomings. One was readily apparent; namely, the anticipated plan to dismiss old troops. Those most learned in military matters saw only with anguish, at the very moment of the admission of the new class, the best trained soldiers, the necessary cadre for the new recruits, broken from the service. Others, in a country obsessed by quantity, envisioned empty regiments, the Army reduced to a skeleton force, the frontier without defense, abandoned to soldiers of a few months training. Because it appeared impossible to explain such a deplorable measure by the sole necessity of realizing a saving of ten to twelve million, it was attributed to an unhealthy pursuit of popularity. Mercier embodied, in the

From Joseph Reinach, *Histoire de l'Affaire Dreyfus*. Vol. I, *Le Procès de 1894* (Paris: Éditions de la Revue Blanche, 1901), pp. 17–21, 23–29, 37–40, 44–50. Translated by the editor.

worst sense of the word, military demagoguery.

The rumor circulated that Germany and Italy would profit from our state of disorganization to try a *coup*. It was an absurd rumor, but it sufficed to rouse the countryside, as well as some garrisons, in the frontier departments.

It was known that the leading members of the Army Committee had loudly voiced their irritation, that the Committee would not wait for the reopening of the Chambers to meet, that it would interpellate the Minister at the first session. It was publicly stated that army inspectors, the chiefs of corps, heard similar opinions expressed at General Headquarters; it was announced that the dismissal of the Minister had been decided upon.

The Army was not sufficiently removed from the nation, the life of the one being too intimately bound to that of the other, for the country not to hear echoes of the conversation exchanged at barracks and at officers' gatherings. The day was to come when a publicist, noted for his keen interest in military affairs, would cry in a reverberating article; "I call on all men of good faith. When the unfortunate Marshal Leboeuf was in power, had the world of generals and colonels ever said of him what is being said today of General Mercier?" Mercier understood that his days were numbered, that he would be sacrificed on the first occasion.

It was then that an anonymous letter arrived at the Ministry of War, one which could have been written only by a French officer, but which had been stolen from the German embassy. That scrap of paper would be his salvation. But at first Mercier saw in it undeniable proof of a mysterious treason and a new source of embarrassment and worry.

When he had first arrived at the Ministry he had been notified by Colonel Sandherr, Chief of Intelligence, that Colonel Schwartzkoppen, at the German embassy, had assumed control of espionage activity. The Italian military attaché, Panizzardi,

worked with his German colleague. Two other spy centers functioned at Strasbourg and Brussels.

The chiefs of staff under the Empire had been violently reproached with the shabbiness of France's espionage service. After the defeat a ridiculous legend attributed the Prussian victory to the work of its spies. Future general staffs were determined to follow the example of Germany. General Mirabel, in particular, had developed the organization called for by his predecessors.

Counter-espionage was the principal wheel of his system. His collaborators in this service, officially entitled "statistical," Colonel Sandherr and Lt. Colonel Cordier, anticipated great results in case of war. They had installed at Brussels an agent named Lajoux, who, being intimately associated with a German agent, Richard Cuers, had pretended to let himself be employed by him and delivered all sorts of watered-down documents. Another agent, Corninge, had been engaged to play the role of "counter-spy" at the expense of the Italian military attaché in Paris. Consequently, a veritable forgery workshop functioned at Headquarters. With the greatest care officers fabricated fake military orders, fake timetables, and fake mobilization plans. There was a closet full of them, carefully accounted for, given the need to have yesterday's false information agree with that of tomorrow. There was also invented imaginary cartridges and other weapons. . . .

The inordinately developed counter-espionage service embodied, furthermore, a double vice. It accustomed officers to making forgeries and tempted certain agents to extend, this time on their own account, their field of operations. The profession was profitable since the spy supped at two tables; he was paid by the employer he served as well as by the one he deceived, but it was all so ignoble that the last traces of conscience had necessarily and quickly to disappear. If the agent believed he was becoming suspect by his correspondent, if he believed himself endangered by carrying too many forged documents, he would bring some real ones to restore the diminished confidence in him. Acquiring a taste for the traffic sometimes sufficed for the spy to slide from counter-espionage to espionage. He was by the very nature of his work in a position to know certain secrets; it seemed foolish not to take advantage of it. Money swindled from a foreigner then ceased to be stolen money; it became the price paid for real treason. . . .

The costly machine had yet other wheels. Sandherr employed a maid in the German embassy. Charged with rough and varied household chores, Mme. Bastian had won the confidence of the ambassador's daughter, the Countess, Marie von Münster. The maid circulated freely in the house and gathered from office drawers and mantel-pieces torn fragments or half-burned letters, notes, and drafts. Once or twice a month she put the booty in a paper bag, then placed the bag where it could be found by an agent named Brücker, who sorted the papers, pasted them back together, and brought them to Captain Rollin at the Statistical Service.

In that sink of spies each suspected his neighbor of treason and accused him of it. Brücker had as his mistress a woman named Forêt, alias Millescamp, who was aware of her lover's profession as well as the extent of his earnings. She had denounced him to Mercier's predecessor, General Loizillon, as a security risk. Brücker had told her, "If the Germans offer me forty or fifty thousand francs, I would not refuse their money." Sometime later he denounced her in turn, accusing her of having stolen one of his notebooks and of delivering it to Schwartzkoppen.

Arrested the 28th of December, 1893, on the charge of spying, Millescamp insisted she was innocent. She claimed Brücker had lost his papers at her home and that she herself had been employed by Captain Rollin to reassure Bastian who, having suddenly taken fright of being discovered and "sent to Siberia," wanted to renounce her trade.

The judges were incredulous at her story, which perhaps was not entirely false, and rushed through her trial. Six days after her arrest she was condemned, at a closed hearing, by the police court to five years imprisonment.

Brücker had told his mistress too many stories. He had told her about the locksmith who provided agents of the service with false keys, and he had acquainted her with his work at the German embassy. He had taken pride in having pasted together the paper, gotten from a wastebasket, that had led to the discovery of the spy Greiner. He had entered the embassy to steal documents. Sandherr judged it prudent to use this fountain of indiscretion at "less delicate" tasks. The rumor was circulated that Brücker had committed suicide, and he no longer acted as intermediary between Bastian and Headquarters. Henceforward, Captain Rollin having left the service, the collector delivered her paper bags directly to Major Henry.

Major Henry was an officer taken from the ranks, not unintelligent, but without scruples or culture, ambitious and compliant. Having entered the service during the last years of the Empire, he had fought and trained for a relatively long time in the lower ranks. He had been attached to the staff of General Mirabel the day that the latter had deemed it wise not to surround himself exclusively with aristocrats. Possessing police instincts, he was promoted for having spied on his colleagues for his chief, who at the time praised his devotion. When Mirabel left the General Staff in 1877 he no longer wished to retain Henry, and placed him in the Statistical Section, then embryonic and directed by Major Campionnet. Held in poor esteem by his superior, he was sent to Africa where he spent ten years in a Zouave regiment. Returning to France in 1891 Henry succeeded, a little later, in re-entering his former office in spite of his professional inadequacy and ignorance of foreign languages. Sandherr had not requested him; he had been imposed by Boisdeffre, with whom he had some contact, and who displayed complete confidence in him.

Henry, installed in the Service, so ingratiated himself with Bastian that she brought her packets to him, not at Headquarters, where the presence of the embassy maid had been suspect, but at nightfall, in lonely places, and usually in churches. With Captain Lauth he made himself responsible for sorting and pasting together the papers, a task which had formerly been that of Brücker and which would have appeared unworthy of officers.

From that time on, Henry sought to exercise control over all activities. Little to the taste of Sandherr and Cordier, he tied himself intimately to Lauth and the archivist Gribelin.

Brücker, meanwhile, criticized for his gossip and humiliated in his self-esteem, and having lost a source of income because of the Millescamp episode, was discontent. The best assignments were those in "the house with the large garden." He complained to the deputy-chief of the Section, Lt. Colonel Cordier, about his reduced role, prowled about the German embassy in disguises, and sought to return to grace by a brilliant *coup*. . . .

Such was, in some of its principal lines, the Statistical Section. Its great vice was its manner of operating as a questionable agency, acquiring base police habits to which too large a number of officers became accustomed and which distorted their intelligence and familiarized them with lies and ruses unworthy of uniform. Its great fault lay in being unable to interpret information. It usually interpreted the documents that fell into its hands in a manner contrary to common sense, displaying neither method, nor critical spirit. In addition, no serious checks were made on the information received; leads failed more than once to achieve results. The Section presented absurd plans, like spreading phylloxera in the vineyards of the Rhine or animal disease in the German cavalry, and became angry when they were rejected by civilian ministries. The Sûreté Générale

(Criminal Investigation Department), if assigned the same work — as it previously had been under Napoleon — would have obtained other results and at less cost. . . .

The letter which was brought to Mercier at the end of September, at a date which can be fixed as Monday, the 24th, read as follows:

I have no news to indicate that you want to see me; however, I am sending you some interesting information.
1. A note on the hydraulic brake of the 120mm. gun and the way in which that part is conducted.
2. A note on the supporting troops. Some modifications will be introduced by the new plan.
3. A note on the modification of artillery formations.
4. A note concerning Madagascar.
5. The provisional Firing Manual for Field Artillery (March 14, 1894).
This last document is extraordinarily difficult to procure, and I have it at my disposal for only a few days. The Minister of War has issued a limited number to the corps, which are responsible for them. Each officer with a copy must send it back after the manoeuvres. If, therefore, you will take notes on what interests you and hold it for me, I shall take it back. That is, unless you want me to have it copied in full and send you the copy. I am going off to manoeuvres.

Mercier was as much irritated as he was excited while reading the document. From the first sentence the letter pointed to an already well-established traffic, which after some interruption by the author, was voluntarily renewed. And since it referred to matters well within the province of the General Staff, the idea immediately arose that the traitor belonged to the Ministry. . . . All the chiefs, from the moment that the *bordereau* was first brought to their attention, viewed it as definite proof that the treason originated at the Ministry of War. At the outset there came the sudden illumination, the absolute conviction, the obsession that the traitor had to be sought among the officers on the General Staff.

The obsession, or perhaps neurosis, was

anchored in the brain and according to some physiological law or other, became exasperated with its own absurdity.

Mercier gave vent to his anger. What! Since January the Statistical Service knew that an officer was working for Schwartz-koppen and that the German attaché received information from the Ministry of War. And for nine months not a sign of a clue. What was the use of the expensive bureau? What was General Gonse doing, the deputy-chief of the General Staff, who was directly responsible? And Boisdeffre himself?

Better than anyone Mercier realized how precarious his political and military position had become. If the treason were noised about and the traitor remained undetected, it would be his *coup de grâce*. The press, the Chambers about to meet, would ascribe the responsibility to him alone. At all costs — you understand, Gonse, and you, Boisdeffre! — the traitor must be found. The area of pursuit is small, limited to the General Staff. Look for him! Find him!

General Boisdeffre claimed that he was "absent when the discovery of the *bordereau* was made." According to Mercier, on the contrary, Henry delivered the document to Colonel Sandherr, "who in turn brought it to General Gonse, General Boisdeffre, and finally to the Minister." A singular contradiction!

As for the manner by which the *bordereau* arrived, Mercier, Gonse, the staff officers, Lauth, Gribelin, everyone except Boisdeffre, who kept silent, and Cordier, who seemed to have had some suspicion, told the same story. "It had been given to Henry by the regular spy at the German embassy," Mme. Bastian, and like all documents coming from her packets, it was "in pieces." And this is Henry's last version: "The *bordereau* was delivered to me. It came by the usual route, with documents whose authenticity is indisputable. Any other version is contrary to truth and physically impossible. . . ."

But all these accounts and all these details, some of which fit together too well

and others not at all, run counter to the fact that the *bordereau*, when Henry received it, was not in pieces, and Henry had no need to restore it. Let us reason and consider. Had Schwartzkoppen thrown into the wastebasket the drafts that he wrote or the insignificant letters he received, he would already be guilty of indiscretion. But a letter like that, announcing and accompanying important documents, the letter of an officer betraying his country! And the letter which he supposedly discarded was not even torn, nor even crumpled. At close examination the artificial character of the tears is apparent. One does not tear a letter like that before disdainfully throwing it into the basket to be emptied by a maid. As long as the paper does not fall into dust it will itself stand as proof that it did not come from the paper bag, that Bastian did not take it from some drawer, and that Schwartzkoppen never received it.

From where did it come? We have observed the agent Brücker, disgraced after the Millescamp affair and complaining of it, seeking to return to favor by no matter what exploit. Audacity proved to be the way. He entered the office of the *concierge* at the German embassy at a time when Bastian was replacing the wife of old Pessin, and there had taken the letter, probably delivered by post, from Schwartzkoppen's box. The latter was then on leave in Berlin; or Bastian, equally willing, gave it to him having stolen it herself. The documents described by the traitor to the Prussian colonel were in another package, one which reached its destination. Brücker opened the envelope, read the letter, and carried his precious windfall to Henry the same day.

Henry had no sooner glanced at it when he recognized the handwriting as that belonging to a friend of twenty years acquaintance, with whom he was close, from whom he had hidden nothing, his former colleague in the same Intelligence Office after 1878, his creditor since 1876, Major Marie-Charles-Ferdinand Walsin-Esterhazy.

Esterhazy had entered the service of

Colonel Schwartzkoppen the previous year. To explain the cause of his treason he had not only alleged, in the letter in which he offered his services, financial difficulties, but being descended from an illustrious Hungarian family, he had never considered himself French. He had told the German attaché that he could take material from the Intelligence Office itself. To prove that he was well situated for spying, he could be seen galloping at the side of a general. Sometimes he amused Schwartzkoppen by the verve of his letters, by his furious invectives against the army chiefs, his hatred and contempt for France. Sometimes he disturbed him because of his manner, his imprudence; his letters were in turn valuable and despicable. He set a high price — 2,000 francs a month — and always begged for more. Treason was mixed with swindling and the Prussian General Staff at times took him for a *provocateur*. Schwartzkoppen had already decided to break with him.

If Henry was the accomplice of Esterhazy, the stolen letter opened an abyss before his feet. If he was not, it told him that his friend was infamous. Having seen the familiar, characteristic handwriting, he behaved like a brother who felt obliged to give warning. Above all, as one of the chiefs of the espionage service, Henry could not remain silent. Even on only a suspicion, he had to avoid a possible chance of error. Whether Henry was the associate of the traitor or simply his friend, was not the simplest recourse to destroy the accusing letter, the one fragile proof?

If the letter had arrived in pieces, in the paper bag, the operation would have indeed been easy and without danger. Bastian was illiterate and enclosed pellmell in packets the scattered fragments she collected, without trying to assemble or read them. No trace, in that case, would remain of the crime. But Brücker knew the value of things, he had read the letter,

estimated the stakes. If Henry had tried to persuade him that it was worthless, fit only to be discarded, the agent, too intelligent, would rebel. He would never allow himself to be deprived of the benefits of the bold action he had just taken. He would speak to Cordier, or to Sandherr, who sometimes looked fixedly at Henry. To destroy the letter was to confess to something other than an unworthy friendship.

On second thought, what risk did Henry run in bringing the letter to Sandherr? The act itself would cover him. Inquiries would be ordered at the Ministry of War, but since Esterhazy was not attached to the General Staff, they would prove useless. After a few days of excitement, in view of the impossibility of finding the culprit at the Ministry, the letter would be filed, would rejoin, in Henry's keeping, the Hypogeum of the archives, with so many other useless papers.

Therefore, Henry did not destroy it; because the letter was intact, however, he tore it to make the initiated believe that it came from the paper bag. He waited for the next shipment of spoils, then, having pasted together the letter, presented it with other documents which legitimately came from Bastian's packets. If it were necessary he could inform his chiefs of Brücker's audacious act and of the ingenious procedure which he himself had found to disguise the inadmissible theft. The envelope had disappeared. The official version would be that the *bordereau*, torn into pieces, "into tiny pieces," came by the usual route. It was a deceitful story because the *bordereau* had been intercepted before arriving at its destination. It was an absurd story, audacious to propose even to fools, because Schwartzkoppen was not in the habit of throwing letters from his spies into the wastebasket.

So began the Affair, with a lie.

Dreyfus Guilty: The Theory of the Jewish Syndicate

HENRI DUTRAIT-CROZON

Dutrait-Crozon was the pseudonym used by two French colonels, Georges Louis Larpent and Frédéric Delebecque. Their 700 page "précis" of the Affair wholly reflects the anti-Dreyfusard position and, accordingly, has been wholly accepted by the anti-Dreyfusards. Although it first appeared in 1909, the second edition, of 1924, has become the definitive one and presents the best summation of the anti-Dreyfusard case. Particular attention, however, should be paid to the type of evidence used by the authors to substantiate their theses.

WELL before Dreyfus was arrested official proof had been obtained that the German and Italian military attachés were personally involved in espionage. On August 30, 1890, an archivist named Boutonnet, in the technical section of the artillery, had been condemned to five years imprisonment for having delivered documents to Germany. The German ambassador, M. von Münster, had given his word of honor that Boutonnet was not in touch with any member of the embassy, but the culprit's confession showed the value of the official denial. M. von Münster then promised that military attachés would in the future refrain from any traffic with French officers or government employees. However, in 1893, one Greiner, in the Ministry of the Marine, was surprised carrying confidential documents at the moment of entering the United States embassy. Greiner was condemned to twenty years hard labor on September 6, 1892, and it was revealed that the German attaché made contact with the traitor by the intermediary of the American attaché, Captain Borup.

The Ministry of War took steps to combat enemy espionage. An annex of the 2nd Bureau of the Army General Staff, officially designated the "Statistical Section," sometimes also referred to as the "Office of Intelligence," was especially concerned with counter-espionage. In 1894 the chief of the Section was Lt. Colonel Sandherr; he was assisted by Major Cordier, Major Henry, Captains Matton and Lauth, and the archivist Gribelin. Colonel Sandherr maintained agents in the enemy camp but, in addition, used "double-agents," that is, agents playing the role of spies and charged with transmitting false information to the military attachés. They brought to the Statistical Section the questions received from the attachés and the Section furnished them with replies, half-true, half-false, or unimportant, but duly controlled by the competent services of the General Staff in order that no information dangerous to the national defense could be communicated.

Moreover, at the German embassy a cleaning woman named Mme. Bastian, referred to as "the usual route," collected papers discarded by the military attaché and forwarded them, in a "packet," to Intelligence. Originally, she had delivered her packets to the agent Brücker; the latter having been "burned," however, in the Millescamp affair, Mme. Bastian worked di-

From Henri Dutrait-Crozon, *Précis de l'Affaire Dreyfus* (Paris: Nouvelle Librairie Nationale, 1924), pp. 5–10, 36–38, 49–50, 102. Translated by the editor.

18

rectly with the officers. At first Captain Rollin received the papers, but after his departure from the service, he was succeeded by Major Henry. The latter sorted them, pasted together those written in French, and gave to Captain Lauth those in a foreign language. The papers, once restored, were given to the chief of the department.

The activities of the military attachés were thus followed very closely, and when, in December, 1893, General Mercier assumed control of the Ministry, Colonel Sandherr was able to make him realize that Schwartzkoppen, the German attaché, and Panizzardi, the Italian, had organized against us a powerful espionage system.

General Mercier received a typical letter, entitled, "the forts of the Meuse," by means of the "usual route" and which had been sent by Schwartzkoppen from Berlin to his intermediary in Paris. General Mercier showed the letter to the President of the Council and Minister of Foreign Affairs, M. Casimir-Périer, and requested that he display it, if necessary, to the German ambassador.

During 1894 Intelligence let it be known that the military attachés had in their pay an officer in the Ministry. The "usual route" had delivered successively:

A telegram of December 25, 1893, sent by the German General Staff to Schwartzkoppen ending with, "anything signed by the General Staff," and the first draft of the latter's response, at the beginning of 1894, in which Schwartzkoppen said that he too had doubts about the authenticity of the documents, but that he was going to forward the letter in which his correspondent had offered to sell his services, and adding that he thought it best not to deal with ordinary officers, that documents were important only if emanating from the Ministry.

A letter of January, 1894, entitled the "Davignon letter," sent by Panizzardi to Schwartzkoppen in which there was mentioned a "friend" of Schwartzkoppen at the Ministry, in Colonel Davignon's office.

A letter of March, 1894, from Panizzardi to Schwartzkoppen in which he said that he received interesting things from their correspondent.

A letter of April, 1894, entitled "that scoundrel D," and concerned with the delivery of staff plans.

Moreover, the Spanish military attaché, the Marquis de Val Carlos, who was in touch with Schwartzkoppen and Panizzardi, in March and April warned a civilian agent named Guénée in French Intelligence, that there was "a wolf in the sheepfold," and in June warned Major Henry that an officer in the 2nd Bureau, or one having been attached to it, worked for the German attaché. Guénée rendered an account of Val Carlos' warnings in two reports, March 28 and April 6, 1894.

This precise information led to an organized surveillance of staff officers. The results were negative.

In the second half of September, the "usual route" brought to Major Henry a packet containing the *bordereau* and five other letters dated the 4th, 21st, 25th, and 26th of August, and the 2nd of September, 1894. Colonel Sandherr received the restored *bordereau* from Major Henry and in turn showed it to Captain Lauth, Captain Matton, and M. Gribelin. . . .

The consensus was that the *bordereau* came from an "artillery officer" and "an officer on the General Staff." "That opinion appeared to me to be evidence itself," declared General Deloye, in charge of artillery, adding, "when I read it I was frightened and said, it is somebody here. . . ."

The investigation was about over when on October 6, Lt. Colonel d'Aboville, deputy-chief of the 4th Bureau, returned from leave. His superior, Colonel Fabré, showed him the photograph of the *bordereau* and Lt. Colonel d'Aboville, basing his reasons on a personal memory and on the nature of the documents listed, which pertained to three different Bureaus of the General Staff, expressed his opinion that the traitor was an artillery officer who had successively belonged to the three Bureaus — that is, a probationer on the General

Staff. While recalling and "discussing" each of the several probationers, the two colonels ascertained that one of them had been poorly evaluated at the 4th Bureau, the artillery captain, Alfred Dreyfus. They then compared his handwriting with that of the *bordereau* and were "stupefied" at the resemblance. But it was only after having pursued their comparative study with documents originating in other bureaus that they decided to inform the deputy-chief of the General Staff to whom they were responsible, General Gonse. He compared the handwriting and in turn informed General Boisdeffre. The latter ordered the comparisons to continue until evening; this was done throughout the afternoon by General Gonse, Colonels Lefort, chief of the 1st Bureau, Boucher, of the 2nd, Fabré, of the 4th, Sandherr, of Intelligence, and only confirmed the first impression. Between five and six P.M. General Boisdeffre was told, and he notified the Ministry.

Meanwhile, Major du Paty de Clam of the 3rd Bureau, who was an amateur graphologist, had been consulted by General Gonse and had given an affirmative opinion; made aware of the seriousness of the affair, however, he asked to resume his examination and only at seven A.M. expressed in a note his opinion that the similarity of handwritings warranted a legal investigation. . . .

The communication of the secret dossier. In the opinion of General Mercier the documents collected by Intelligence and which demonstrated the internal operation of foreign espionage, constituted appreciable elements of which the judges ought to be aware, but he decided to limit communication of them to the judges alone because he considered a secret trial no sufficient guarantee of security, and that the least indiscretion would renew the danger of rupture with Germany, so narrowly avoided December 12. At the time war would have been declared in unfavorable conditions; Germany had preceded us in the refabrication of artillery *matériel,* we were in the process of revising our mobilization plans, we were ignorant of the intentions of the new emperor of Russia (Alexander III had just died); in short, the outbreak of war would put us in a very unfortunate position. General Mercier, moreover, could not forget the observations of M. Hanotaux on the origins of the *bordereau* and, if this document could be introduced into the proceedings without disclosing its source, other secret documents, bluntly accusing the attachés of espionage, could not be.

The Ministry had compiled for its personal use, a commentary on the secret documents, written by Colonel Sandherr and Major du Paty de Clam. The commentary analyzed three documents — Schwartzkoppen's draft, the Davignon letter, the "scoundrel D" letter relative to staff plans and established the following: 1. that there had been leaks in the Ministry, 2. that the leaks originated within the General Staff, 3. that they had successively taken place in different Bureaus, and 4. that they could have been the work of Dreyfus. The three documents in question, the commentary on them, a summary of the statements of Val Carlos, and documents for purposes of comparison constituted the secret dossier which, in the opinion of the judges, would necessarily authenticate Major Henry's deposition by furnishing proofs to support it, except that which concerned the actual naming of Dreyfus, a designation made by Major Henry on the basis of his own authority and as a result of his private information.

The secret dossier was placed in an envelope carrying the inscription, "To the President of the court-martial, to be opened during deliberations for any useful purpose." It was delivered to Colonel Maurel by Major du Paty de Clam, who told the Colonel that the envelope within contained a special reference. The reference, in the opinion of the Ministry, constituted a "moral order" to take cognizance of the dossier. The envelope was opened at the time of deliberation. Its contents hardly influenced the judges; their conviction was obtained from the arguments presented. . . .

The period following the condemnation of Dreyfus included the simultaneous manoeuvers of Mathieu Dreyfus, Picquart, and Esterhazy. The Jews wanted the Ministry of War to take the initiative in revision; Picquart was therefore instructed to get his superiors to substitute Esterhazy for Dreyfus. That substitution, however, was possible only under two conditions: it was necessary for Esterhazy to have a handwriting identical to that of the *bordereau,* and it was necessary to make it appear that he had been in a position to be familiar with the documents listed in it, the documents having been in the hands only of an officer on the General Staff, or one closely associated with it.

The connivance of Esterhazy with the Jews was therefore indispensable for the success of the plan. Esterhazy in fact applied himself to model his handwriting on that of a facsimile of the *bordereau* which he was given; he also tried to have himself assigned to the Ministry of War and sought there a position "in any office whatever." If he had succeeded in these attempts he would have been able subsequently to demonstrate, with more likelihood of success than if he had not, previous contact with officers of the Ministry. Thanks to these connections he would have been able in 1894 to obtain access to the materials listed in the *bordereau.*

The beginning of the steps taken by Esterhazy coincide with the moment when Picquart related the account of his investigation of Esterhazy to General Boisdeffre. The press campaign that Mathieu had arranged to intimidate the Minister of War and the Chief of Staff, coincided in turn with Picquart's attempt to substitute Esterhazy for Dreyfus.

The first step taken by Esterhazy to enter the Ministry came at the end of July, 1896. Picquart told Boisdeffre of his suspicions on August 5, 1896. Picquart's note stating his conviction of Dreyfus' innocence was sent September 1, 1896. The beginning of the press campaign undertaken by Mathieu was September 3, 1896. It is entirely probable, moreover, that Picquart and Esterhazy, although both apparently obeying the same hidden orders, acted without knowledge of each other.

It is equally remarkable that the role played by Esterhazy was not really as dangerous for him than might be at first thought. His manoeuvers, which tended to create the impression that he had committed the crime for which Dreyfus had been condemned, would evidently bring him before a court-martial. But given the unanimous belief in Dreyfus' guilt on the part of the Army and the public, he could certainly count on acquittal. Given, furthermore, the weakness of the charges which could be invoked and the manner of their presentation, acquittal seemed all the more certain.

The anticipated acquittal once obtained, Esterhazy would be able, fully secure, to continue openly his activities in favor of Dreyfus, even to declare that he had written the *bordereau.* He would thus serve the Jews by allowing them to accuse the General Staff of having committed a first crime in having knowingly condemned an innocent Dreyfus, and then a second in knowingly having acquitted a guilty Esterhazy. . . .

The court refrained from citing the decisive objections which have been made to the "confession" of Esterhazy concerning the *bordereau;* that he had modeled his handwriting on a bad facsimile given to him, in such a way that he had introduced into his handwriting all the blemishes of the reproduction, and not existing in the original. The court was not ignorant of these objections, which had been made by two witnesses, Colonel du Paty and M. Henri Rochefort; likewise it had received three accounts of the imposture of Esterhazy. *The court left this point in the dark, not even wishing to point out to the public the thesis of "Esterhazy, straw man of the Jews," which is the key to the Dreyfus affair.*

The Syndicate. From its beginning the Dreyfusard campaign appeared so well-organized that public opinion did not hesitate to believe in the existence of an organizing "syndicate." The publication of a considerable number of propaganda placards, brochures, and books, the creation of several newspapers that were born and died with the affair (*Droits de l'homme, Volonté, Petit Bleu,* etc.), all demanded financial resources. Ministers have always denied ever having received prefectural reports about foreign contributions entering France. M. de Freycinet, however, told General Jamont, following his resignation, that the government was aware of 35 million having entered France coming from Germany and England. M. de Freycinet plainly stated at Rennes that our agents' reports about foreign propaganda expressed reservations only about the amount. At the time of the second revision, however, he said that the government had found no trace of such facts and that General Jamont had misunderstood the sense of his words.

General Zurlinden reported having had information from diverse sources about contributions organized in France and abroad by rabbis in favor of Dreyfus. In addition, there had previously been published the manifesto of a Committee of Defense Against Anti-semitism from which it was learned that the Committee had taken an active but "discreet" part in the Dreyfusard campaign. It had been founded at the time of Dreyfus' condemnation, on January 10, 1895, on the initiative of the chief rabbi, Zadoc Kahn, and had as president, the head of the Alliance Isréalite universelle, Narcisse Leven, born in Rhennish Prussia, of a Prussian father. . . .

Certain attempts at corruption are positive: of the paleographer, M. Bouton, of M. Mertian de Muller, of the political grouping of the radical left presided over by M. Dujardin-Beaumetz. Bernard Lazare, furthermore, in November, 1896, declared to M. Rochefort that all the financial sacrifices necessary would be made in order to have the innocence of Dreyfus proclaimed, and M. Rochefort told how bankrupt newspapers suddenly had found themselves in a very prosperous position. The Marquis de Maussabré told the Marquis de Grandmaison that he heard from Rothschild that the Jews were subsidizing socialist and revolutionary newspapers. Finally, Joseph Reinach had *Le Figaro* at his disposal, as M. de Rodays has testified.

Later, in 1907, Gustave Hervé reproached Picquart, who became Minister, with having "cashed the same paycheck as himself." In 1908, in the Chamber, a letter was read from a former editor of *L'Aurore* and *Le Temps Nouveaux,* revealing that bands of anarchists were enrolled to serve as escorts to Picquart at public meetings during the first revisionist campaign. . . .

Because they saw that the public was still hostile, the Jews postponed the attempt to rehabilitate Dreyfus and kept the affair from the elections of 1902. The way was prepared, however, by attacking the Catholic Church and the Army — both of which had opposed revision — and by seeking new evidence. Reprisals were undertaken against the Army, and the mission of purifying it entrusted to General André. . . .

Finally, Esterhazy died rich, while in 1897 he had enormous debts and had even been unable to travel, two years later, from England to Rennes. . . .

M. Jacques Bonzon, "a whole-hearted Dreyfusard from the very beginning," wrote in 1911 that the Syndicate was "a reality. . . ."

The German Explanation:
Schwartzkoppen's Notebooks

MAXIMILIAN VON SCHWARTZKOPPEN

Lt. Colonel von Schwartzkoppen became first military attaché in 1891 and was serving in that capacity when the Dreyfus Affair began. He returned to Germany November 15, 1897, at the time Mathieu Dreyfus denounced Esterhazy. Although repeatedly asked to confirm Esterhazy's guilt, Schwartzkoppen kept silent. As a general, he was wounded on the Russian front and died in a Berlin military hospital January, 1917. The preceding month, however, on his deathbed and in the presence of his wife, he proclaimed the innocence of Dreyfus. To justify his conduct, he had written in 1903 an account of his experiences as attaché until November, 1896. His widow published this account under the title, "Die Wahrheit über Dreyfus" in 1930 and it was translated — with some letters demonstrating the pressure exerted on Schwartzkoppen not to speak — into French the same year.

Oɴ July 20, between three and four o'clock in the afternoon, a Frenchman called on me at the military office of the German embassy in Paris (78 rue de Lille) and had himself announced by the office boy, Auguste Burde, as coming to ask about a passport. This was not unusual because at that time a passport was still necessary for Alsace-Lorraine, and every French officer who wanted to go there on leave had to obtain authorization from the *Statthalterschaft* in Strasbourg. Such authorization was frequently refused; that is why French officers often asked the intervention of the German military attaché.

I requested that the visitor enter and a few instants later, a gentleman whom I at once recognized as a French officer in civilian clothing entered the room. He was forty-two or forty-five years of age, of medium height, was delicate and weak looking, had a sinewy face with deeply socketed black eyes, carefully arranged and graying hair, and a military salt-and-pepper moustache. On the button-hole of

his black overcoat he wore the red ribbon of the Legion of Honor. While entering the room he seemed ill-at-ease and somewhat embarrassed; his somber and inquiring glance surveyed the room to make certain that I was alone.

When I asked the reason for his visit, he introduced himself as an officer on the General Staff in active service, constrained by necessity to take a step which would render him contemptible in my eyes, but about which he had done much thinking and which he was forced to take in order to save his wife and children from misery and certain ruin. Unfavorable circumstances, unfortunate speculations, and his wife's illness had placed him in a difficult economic situation and, in order to retain for his family a small piece of property that he possessed near Châlons, it was necessary to obtain money at all costs. Each of his attempts to do it in an honest and legal way had failed; only one solution remained, to offer his services to the German General Staff, in the hope that by so doing he

From *Les Carnets de Schwartzkoppen: La Vérité sur Dreyfus* (Paris: Éditions Rieder n.d.), pp. 5–13, 15, 19–22, 24, 161–162, 323–325. Translated by the editor.

would quickly find himself able to meet his various obligations. He had seriously reflected; it offered the only way out that was still open to him; if he failed, he would have to shoot himself. But the thought of his sick wife and his children had so far prevented him from taking this extreme decision, although he was readily aware that it was the best solution. He was perfectly capable of rendering important services, because he had spent considerable time in Algeria and was completely informed about military conditions in that country; he had also spent much time at the Italian frontier and was thoroughly familiar with the frontier defenses; during 1881 and 1882 he had worked at the Intelligence Office of the Ministry of War. He was closely associated with Colonel Sandherr, Chief of Intelligence, and was an old school-mate of President Casimir-Périer. He was also the friend of the deputy Jules Roche, who had promised to appoint him second in command in the event the latter became Minister of War. At the moment he was stationed outside Paris, but in a short while would return and renew the various relationships previously had with the Ministry of War. In a few days he was to attend very important military manoeuvers at Châlons. To prove that he already possessed important information, he took from an inside pocket a paper with writing on it which he gave me to read.

I was extremely surprised and shocked by that offer — an officer on the General Staff in active service who did not hesitate to betray his country, and who bluntly asked a member of his profession, like a friend, to serve as his intermediary. I replied, while returning his paper unread, that it was in no way my role to assist an officer from the path of duty and honor, and that I could only advise him to renounce his plan, to turn around, to forget and let me forget the step he had taken. He thereupon answered that he had carefully considered his act, that he was well aware it would make him a "scoundrel," but that he could no longer draw back.

If I showed him the door he would try in another way to take advantage of what he knew, because he absolutely needed to obtain money, etc. Once again I directed his attention to the immorality of his plan and dismissed him saying that, in my position I was unable to interest myself in such offers. After that he took leave of me stating that he would return in a few days.

The following day, July 21, I received a letter from the person in question, in which he wrote, "I am leaving very shortly on the trip which I told you about," and adding that, thanks to his family relations, he would equally be able to furnish me with some important information about Russia.

On July 22 I related the story of his visit to Berlin Intelligence and received, on the 26th, the reply to pursue negotiations with him.

On July 27, without having notified me, he returned to my office and introduced himself as Major Count Walsin-Esterhazy, battalion commander in the 74th Infantry Regiment at Rouen. He told me that his wife was born de Nettancourt-Vaubécourt, owner in her own right of the chateau of Dammartin near Sainte-Menehould, in the Department of the Marne, and related to families like Clermont-Tonnèrre and Banfrémont. To prove his sincerity he produced the Table of Mobilization of his regiment and asked to be remunerated at 2,000 francs a month. I tried yet once more to persuade the Major and make him see the monstrousness of his action. He maintained that he had well considered, that he was forced to do it, and that if I did not accept his offer, he would go elsewhere.

To comply with the wishes of Intelligence, I then suggested that the Major put himself directly in rapport with it; I wanted to know nothing about the affair. He absolutely rejected that proposal, alleging that such affairs could be negotiated only between two persons, face to face, and that any third party constituted a danger. To be in direct rapport with me presented no risk because no one would believe him capable of doing anything of that nature. He could see me alone, at the embassy, and would attract no attention because a crowd of people entered and left daily. I dismissed the Major by telling him I could not accept his offer and begged him yet once more to give up his scheme. He withdrew leaving the Table of Mobilization, saying that he would reclaim it on another visit.

I estimated that the proper thing to do was relate the whole story to the Chief of Intelligence, and if that proved impossible, to the Chief of Staff. In reply to my request, I was told that the former would be on leave at Michelstadt in the Odenwald and that I could find him there. I arrived August 3, 1894, and the next day obtained from Major Müller, then in charge of Intelligence, the interview I wanted. The result was that he advised me to put myself in rapport with a source of information that could be of great value if it were proven that important documents could be expected. But in the contrary case, it would be necessary to end all rapport at once. A fixed sum, payable every month, could not be promised. An appreciation of the value of the information would be left to me. . . .

Thus I crossed the threshold fully aware of the heavy responsibility which I had undertaken. I took that decision because I believed that in the interest of the Army, it was my duty to do so, but I fully realized the danger of my position and that, as a Prussian officer, I had been placed in an extremely disagreeable position.

On September 1st, 1894, Esterhazy presented himself at my office at 6:30 P.M. In an hour and a half of conversation he gave me much interesting news as well as the following documents: 1. A list of supporting troops, 2. a description of the 120 medium range cannon, and 3. an outline of the Manual of Field Artillery Fire. He also told me that the Madagascar expedition was decided on. Then he said he was going to mass artillery manoeuvers at the Sis-

sonne camp (in the *bordereau*: "I am going on manoeuvers") and would soon communicate his observations. I personally received this report from Esterhazy September 5th, and on the 6th, in the form of a letter sent to the embassy, a report on the proposed Madagascar expedition.

I give all these dates and submit a complete enumeration of the documents because they form the point of departure of the famous "Dreyfus Affair." The forwarding of the documents of September 1st had been preceded by the depositing of the *bordereau* with the embassy *concierge*, the latter having occurred between August 16 and September 1. . . .

The consequence of all this is that the *"bordereau"* had NEVER BEEN in my hands, that it was left by Esterhazy between August 16 and September 1 before his departure for manoeuvers, and that before it reached me, it had been taken by a third party and brought to French Intelligence. Strangely enough, there had never been mention of the document between Esterhazy and myself, so that I only learned of its existence in 1896, when its facsimile appeared in *Le Matin.* Esterhazy had naturally thought that the *bordereau* reached its destination. It has never been definitely established who delivered it to French Intelligence; however, after all that was learned about the espionage carried on by Mme. Bastian, employed by the embassy as a cleaning woman, there could be no doubt about her collaboration. . . . That the *bordereau* was not found in the wastebasket follows from the fact that I had never received it. Mme. Bastian or some secret agent necessarily found it in my box at the *concierge's* office, and in order to make it appear that it came from my wastebasket, tore it into tiny pieces. As for the old *concierge*, Pessin, as well as his wife, English by birth, I am convinced that they had absolutely no part in any of that affair. . . .

A very important event for the subsequent development of the Dreyfus Affair was the publication by *Le Matin* (November 10, 1896) of the facsimile of the *bordereau*, made possible by the forwarding of its photograph by the handwriting expert, Teyssonnières. He was one of the experts called by the Ministry of War to the council which tried Dreyfus. The publication aroused great emotion throughout all France, but the greatest was probably mine and Esterhazy's, because it was ONLY THEN that it became clear that Dreyfus had been confused for Esterhazy, and as a result, condemned in his place. As for Esterhazy, from the moment his handwriting was published, he realized that he was lost. I immediately recognized his handwriting in the facsimile and at once informed my friend Panizzardi of it, to whom FOR THE FIRST TIME I then disclosed the name and position of my correspondent.

My situation became extremely painful. The question rose before me whether I ought not proclaim the whole truth in order to correct the terrible error and thus bring about the liberation of an innocent convict. If I had been free to act as I would have wished, I certainly would have done it. On examining things more closely, however, I decided not to mix in the affair because, in the given conditions, I would not have been believed anyway; moreover, diplomatic considerations opposed such an action. The realization, furthermore, that the French Government was in the process of taking the necessary measures to spread light and redress the injustice, served to strengthen my decision. . . .

[The following advice was sent to Schwartzkoppen by Prince Hohenlohe, son of the Chancellor, when it was learned that Schwartzkoppen had requested to be allowed to clear Picquart, who had been accused of forging the petit-bleu.] *Editor's note.*

. . . Let us admit, for example — I am only formulating an hypothesis — that you write a letter to the President of the Council of War, something as follows: "You are a soldier like me; you will therefore understand why I feel obliged to tell you on my honor that the *petit-bleu* sent to Esterhazy is not a forgery, but was written by me. Signed, Schwartzkoppen."

What would be the impression created by that letter, or one like it? In my humble opinion, an excellent one. Yes, in my opinion, you would be the most popular man, and the German Government, the most popular government in France. But for how long? That is another question. Because what lasts for any time in France? Certainly for twenty-four hours and even for a few days, and consequently there would no longer be a Picquart Affair, and he would be brilliantly acquitted.

In the contrary case, if Picquart is condemned, his condemnation would give birth to a new Dreyfus affair, now called the Picquart affair, and to a new campaign for revision, perhaps even more violent than the first. Anarchy, struggle, and discord would only grow in France, the Army would be perhaps still more discredited and how it will all end, no one can foresee. We can observe it all quietly as disinterested spectators, remaining entirely passive and awaiting the end of the whole tragedy. This is the second possible attitude.

Would it be, from a purely political point of view, more profitable for Germany? I think it would.

Pardon me if I make you lose precious time by these wordy considerations. Do not blame me for them. I have felt myself able — in view of our old friendship — to suggest these thoughts in a way wholly devoid of pretension. . . .

I would be grateful to you for briefly acknowledging receipt of this letter.

Yours always devotedly,
A. HOHENLOHE

II. THE UNENDING CONFLICT

The Affair as a Conspiracy

JACQUES KAYSER

Like some other Frenchmen who write history, Jacques Kayser worked as a newspaperman and was actively involved in politics. He was former editor of *La République*, was on the staff of *Le Monde*, and served as Secretary-General of the Radical-Socialist Party. He has written histories of Radicalism, of the provincial press during the Third Republic, and a life of Lafayette. His history of the Dreyfus Affair demonstrates how strongly some present-day writers still regard an Army-Church conspiracy and anti-semitism as providing the keys to the background of the Affair.

THE Dreyfus Affair is something more than a trial of exceptional character. Through its reactions on politics, both national and international, it constitutes an important chapter in the history of France.

Twenty-four years after the foundation of the Third Republic it let loose a flood of events which placed the new order for a moment in jeopardy; but by the final triumph of justice, which was the triumph of all who had the Republic truly at heart, that order was placed on a surer basis.

Child of defeat on the field of battle, the Third Republic enthroned itself on the ruins of the Empire, and reaped advantage from its unpopularity. But France as a whole was not yet ripe for republican ideas. The Republic was accepted by many as an arrangement merely transitional, and its infancy was passed in an atmosphere of latent hostility. Its enemies were in the majority, but the liquidation of the war of 1870, the events of the Commune, the necessities imposed by a drastic peace treaty, and the resolute effort of reconstruction drove political differences for the time being into the background.

If those who desired the restoration of the Empire were only a handful, there were vast numbers who desired the restoration of the monarchy. But they were divided on the question of who should be the future king of France, and their division was the Republic's opportunity.

Placed at the head of the executive, Thiers ruled as a republican; but it was his opinion that the Republic must be conservative or cease to be, and events seemed to justify him.

Indeed, when the popularly elected National Assembly was called upon to pass judgment on the new constitutional laws which were deemed necessary for France, and to decide on the form of government, there was a majority of one vote, and of one only, in favour of republicanism. In other words the Third French Republic, established under such conditions, was firmly bound in the chains which its origin and the compromise resulting from that first vote imposed on it, and had eventually to free itself from them.

The Republic was thus insecure. The clumsiness and violence of the President,

From Jacques Kayser, *The Dreyfus Affair* (N.Y., 1931), pp. 7–11. Reprinted by permission of Crown Publishers, Inc. Translated by Nora Bickley.

Marshal MacMahon, who on 16th May, 1877, attempted a sort of *coup d'état* against the Chamber of Deputies, were necessary to confirm it.

That bid for personal power fused the Republicans into unity and established the parliamentary régime which, by its system of direct representation, became the organ of the will of the people.

The Republic had tottered. Once victorious, it gathered strength and became the rallying-point of the forces of France. The Republic was governed by republicans for republicans. Important legislative measures gave concrete expression to the desire and need of reform in every direction.

The Republic struck deep roots in the country. At every election the republican majority increased. The parties in opposition were crumbling. Since the death of the Prince Imperial the Bonapartists had been reduced to silence. The monarchists, divided among themselves and incapable of effective action, made but a show of interference. The Right was no longer led by the enemies of the régime but by those who asserted, as Thiers had done, that the Republic ought to remain conservative, and their influence, feeble in politics, was only effective in public life, among the middle classes, and in the world of finance. The Left, on the other hand, was active and of growing power in the country. It asserted its pretensions and its rights and proclaimed its faith in a Republic boldly radical.

Meanwhile the stability of France was subjected to influences and rivalries which put it in constant peril. A nationalist movement took shape, a protest against the policy of carrying out the Treaty of Versailles in 1871. The younger generation was ready for mischief. The League of Patriots, whose object was to foment the spirit of militarism and disseminate the cult of Vengeance, intensified its propaganda and worked up a dangerous agitation. General Boulanger, the Minister for War, by pandering to the passions of the chauvinists and playing the demagogue, gained no little popularity. An incident on the Franco-German frontier (the Schnaebele affair) made the situation more acute. The position of Boulanger, the "general of the *Revanche*," was strengthened by it, and demonstrations in his support were organized up and down a country seething with excitement.

In Parliament parties were in confusion. The Government, in despair, tried to discover a basis of agreement and tentatively initiated a policy of pacification. But a new crisis arose, the result of a scandal in which the son-in-law of the President of the Republic was implicated. It had to do with the sale of honours; the malcontents made the most of it; and it ended in the resignation of President Grévy.

"The Republic," it was said, "is the rule of nepotism and corruption." To the diatribes of the press was added the clamour of public meetings; and all the energy, skill, and integrity of the new republican leaders were needed to stand firm against this double attack, now consolidated into one, of the Nationalists and the Boulangists.

At last, however, it seemed that the Republic, which had gained strength at the new elections, was really on the point of inaugurating an era of peace and victorious prosperity. But a fresh scandal shook the régime to its foundations. This was the Panama affair, a case of corruption in which a large number of members of Parliament were involved and compromised. What a weapon this placed in the hands of those whose dream it was to destroy the Republic, and who accused the Government of complicity in dubious undertakings, may easily be imagined. But by now the new order had struck deep roots in the soil of the country, and this perilous ordeal served as a touchstone of the soundness of its institutions.

Nevertheless, this was a time of increasing social trouble. The first great strikes were coincident with the growth of the Socialist party which Jaurès was leading into battle. From the benches of Parliament and from the columns of the press the militants sent forth their rallying cry, and the swollen ranks of their effectives became a force in the Opposition.

Besides these concerted movements, the individual acts of anarchists spread terror through Paris. To draw attention to social injustice by shocking public opinion they multiplied their outrages, and devoted themselves to direct propaganda by deed. The assassination of the President of the Republic, Sadi-Carnot, was the culmination of their efforts, which were carried on to the accompaniment of the cry, "Society is rotten."

Thus at the beginning of 1894 the situation was fraught with trouble. The Republic was in being; it had gained strength. But morally it was compromised and the balance of parties was difficult to maintain. The Government could introduce no measure of reform which did not dissatisfy its supporters, and found itself driven to a policy of conflict. The union of republicans which had been formed in the hour of danger existed no longer. The Socialists, the vanguard of democracy, fought no longer for the Republic and were intent only on the defence of their own obvious class interests.

A reactionary nationalist movement was taking shape, directed at once outwards against the foreigner, and especially against Germany, and inwards against the Jew, represented as a profiteer and the agent of the foreigner, and the Socialist as the creator of disorder. The army seemed to be the citadel of order. Its head, General Mercier, was obsessed by the transient glory of Boulanger and dreamed of popularity. The two great forces of resistance to democratic progress were the Church and the Army. They were in direct collusion. The generals and the bishops were leagued in their determination to thwart the work of republican action. They were in a communion of hatred against Liberalism and the Jews. Beneath their common preoccupations were manifest the unwearying efforts of the Jesuits, those implacable and irreconcilable enemies of modern and republican ideas.

With the Republicans at loggerheads and public opinion in a state of flux, troubled and at a loss, the army and the clergy believed that the moment had come to launch a great offensive, hoping thereby to regain their grip on the country, which since 1870, and more especially since 1878, they had let slip from their control.

A case of treason gave them the opportunity which they sought; and the Dreyfus Affair was therefore no mere case for the Courts — "the great Jewish conspiracy to deliver France to the enemy" — but the most momentous political battle which the reactionary and clerical parties of the Right, in full panoply and at full strength and aided by all their technical resources have waged against the Republic.

Dreyfus Guilty:
The Classical Conservative Interpretation

JACQUES BAINVILLE

Bainville wrote extensively on French history in a characteristically concise and terse style. His views are conservative, and he contributed numerous political and economic articles to the monarchist and nationalist *Action Française*. Because of his histories, particularly the works on France and on Napoleon, he was elected to the *Académie Française* in 1935, the year before his death. The following passages, taken from his history of the Third Republic, present the best-balanced conservative interpretation of the Dreyfus Affair.

The Dreyfus Affair lasted twelve years. It took Joseph Reinach six volumes to tell the story. The simple *Précis* of Dutrait-Crozon contains seven hundred pages. There have been countless incidents, episodes, law-suits growing out of law-suits, and dramatic rebounds, while soldiers, lawyers, magistrates, experts, spies, ministers, diplomats, writers, maids, and even a former head of state, in all almost a thousand persons, intervened as actors or as witnesses. The complexity reached such a point that one humorously distinguished among bachelors, masters, and doctors of Dreyfusology. One no longer spoke of the Dreyfus Affair, but the Affair, the great, the only one, which raised Frenchmen against each other and preoccupied them for years. In order to understand its extraordinary scope, it is indispensable to recall the circumstances in which it was born, grew, then coiled on itself to such a degree that, no longer capable of resolution, it had to be cut off, as in Turkey, where according to Montesquieu, the method of ending disputes is immaterial, provided that they are ended.

In relating the origins of the Dreyfus Affair, the reader will take note of its location in that part of the narrative where the republicans carry out the reorganization of the Army. They had created a military instrument capable of resisting Germany. It was natural for Germany to be disturbed, for her to seek knowledge of the plans of the French General Staff and of our secret armaments. Germany began to expand espionage activity the day that Freycinet set himself to work. Two traitors had already been discovered and condemned; one, named Boutonnet, an archivist in the technical department of the Artillery, the other, Greiner, a naval clerk. At the Ministry of War the Intelligence Service was on the watch. It did not doubt that the German military attaché, Schwartzkoppen, in liaison with the Italian attaché, Panizzardi, had established an espionage agency at the German embassy.

There was also at the German embassy a cleaning woman, Mme. Bastian, who gathered papers from wastebaskets, slipped them under her petticoat and forwarded them to the Ministry of War without even knowing their nature because she was illiterate. It was thus, that in the second half of September, 1894, there arrived at the Intelligence Service a torn and crumpled

From Jacques Bainville, *La Troisième République* (Paris, 1935), pp. 194–203, 204–208, 211–213, 216–219. Reprinted by permission of the Librairie Arthème Fayard. Translated by the editor.

letter the author of which announced the delivery of documents concerned with the national defense and which was called the *"bordereau."* This piece of paper was to rouse France. Fewer calamities had emerged from Pandora's box than from Schwartzkoppen's wastebasket.

It is important to note, in the first place, that the authenticity of the *bordereau* was never contested. Without ever having been questioned it constituted the substance of the offense about which one fought for twelve years. Its origin, in fact, was indisputable. But because the document emanated from a theft committed at the German embassy, it was of a nature to create serious complications. For that reason General Saussier and the Minister of Foreign Affairs, Hanotaux, wished to prevent the opening of legal proceedings. The government held a contrary opinion, based on the observation that impunity encouraged treason and that it was necessary to set an example. William II, moreover, had already complained that his military attaché was implicated by the French press, and he demanded a note disengaging the responsibility of the ambassador. The removal of documents from the inviolable domicile of a diplomatic representative was sufficient to create a major incident. An "historic night" took place at the Élysée when it was feared that, because of the above, Germany would declare war on France, a circumstance which served all the more to prove the authenticity of the *bordereau.*

At first, no one in particular was suspected. It appeared that the writer of the *bordereau* was an artillery officer and associated with the General Staff. The list of documents sent to Schwartzkoppen led to direct inquiries among the probationers who necessarily passed through all divisions. Finally, proceeding by elimination, a resemblance of handwritings implicated Captain Alfred Dreyfus. He was condemned by a court-martial without there having been a *fragante delicto,* without a confession having been recorded by the investigation or by the tribunal. The defense attorney had therefore pleaded not guilty. Explanations amounting to a confession made by Dreyfus at the degradation ceremony were afterwards contested.

It was soon maintained that Dreyfus had been condemned only after secret documents were delivered to his judges and because he was Jewish. The court-martial was suspected of having yielded to the summonses of an anti-semitic newspaper. But the court did not institute itself. The Government of 1894, furthermore, had accepted its verdict and thus committed the original error. The wrong, if one considers the injuries France was to endure, lay in the repeal of a judgment; it was that which made the affair a controversy. It would have been more prudent to watch Dreyfus until he was caught in the act. It would have been easier, and less honest, to get rid of him without leaving traces. A General Staff devoid of scruples would have silently sent him to one of the colonies from which one does not return.

Soon after the trial of 1894, his brothers, after having defended him, undertook the task of establishing his innocence. Devoted, tenacious, and possessing relations and resources, they interested several persons in the cause of their kinsman. Some sensitive or generous souls were troubled by the assertion that an injustice had been committed. Others — this was the example of Péguy — made the reparation of the injustice a question of conscience and honor for the French. It was in the hope of cutting short budding agitation that Méline invoked the principle of the "rendered judgment." In order to break the verdict of 1894 it was necessary to produce new evidence. While waiting for it to be found, it was claimed that an innocent Dreyfus had been unjustly condemned and by illegal methods, although, as an example of many strange contradictions, partisans of innocence as ardent as Jaurès and Trarieux admitted the necessity of secret documents in a treason trial. But it was added that they had been delivered in bad faith, which led to the making of generalizations.

Courts-martial, officers, their loyalty, their hierarchy, the Army itself, sacred to most Frenchmen, were all censured. The Affair broke out of its juridical limits. Those involved placed themselves into one of two camps. That of the partisans of innocence was at first extremely unpopular, and this very consideration was not unfavorable to the Dreyfusard cause. If courage was then necessary to rally to it, it had attracted originality, defiance of public opinion, sacrifice itself. The first Dreyfusards proudly called themselves intellectuals. Later, they tried to separate themselves from eleventh hour workers, from the crowd that invaded their chapel when there were only advantages to gain by so doing.

Ideas carried along a movement. The Affair remained stalemated. The moment a crime was acknowledged and accusative documents existed, there had to be someone to commit it. If the author of the *bordereau* was not Dreyfus, who was he? Mathieu Dreyfus denounced the infantry Major, Esterhazy, a man lost in debts and deprived of honor, whose guilt was also insisted on by the new head of the Intelligence Service, Major, later Lt. Colonel, Picquart. This led to new complications because Picquart, in turn, was accused of intrigue and forgeries for which he was prosecuted, while he himself accused his colleagues of forgeries and prevarications. In the meantime, Esterhazy having been accused, was arraigned before a court-martial. He declared himself innocent. Although everything about him was ambiguous, his accusers lacked proof and the investigation revealed nothing. The government abandoned the prosecution. Esterhazy was acquitted to the frantic applause of the public. It was believed that this was the end of the Affair. Actually it was the beginning.

The veritable signal for retaking the field was given by a newspaper founded to support the Dreyfusard cause and edited by Clemenceau. On January 13, 1898, two days after the acquittal of Esterhazy, *L'Aurore* published under the title "I ac-cuse" a violent statement signed by Émile Zola. Anatole France correctly said that it was "a revolutionary act of incomparable power." Zola accused the military chiefs and judges of having willingly destroyed an innocent man and deliberately whitewashing a guilty one. He, in turn, was prosecuted for defamation and injuries at the court of assizes and condemned. Excitement in the two camps intensified. On both sides positions were taken. The point was passed where it was possible to proceed to a demonstration capable of convincing both parties.

With the exoneration of Esterhazy, a strange situation ensued. The law states that an accused man, having benefitted from a verdict of acquittal, can never be prosecuted or indicted again for the same crime, whether his guilt is a hundred times proven, whether his confession is the most complete. After his acquittal, Esterhazy gave to understand, at first not without precautions and reservations, then in an increasingly clear manner, that he had written the *bordereau*. In the absence of risk and sanctions these confessions were held suspect. The anti-Dreyfusards contested that Esterhazy had been in a position to procure the documents described in the *bordereau*. And could not a man as blemished as he was assume the guilt in order to render service to another? If he was capable of treason, he was also easily capable of substituting himself for a traitor. The mystery was not dispelled and new elements worsened the situation. The Dreyfusards, while making full use of Esterhazy's confession, also believed it necessary to support it with the testimony of handwriting experts, and the latter were no more infallible than those who recognized the hand of Dreyfus in the accusing document. Whatever he may have done, if even Esterhazy had been wrongly exonerated, his case could no longer be the object of the contradictory judgment alone necessary to dispel obscurities and doubts. On his part, on the contrary, the condemned Dreyfus would have to be judged again if evidence of a nature to establish his innocence was revealed. The Affair became inextricable.

It provoked growing violence on both sides and was transformed into an instrument of civil war, which made Charles Maurras say that if Dreyfus were innocent it was necessary to name him marshal of France and shoot a dozen of his principal defenders. Those who had been pushed aside by the new course taken by the regime, those who aspired to return to truly republican ideas, those who were anarchists by temperament or by profession, ranged themselves little by little on the side of Dreyfus. The first champions of innocence had acted alone. Interested or disinterested in the cause, they had suffered for it, exposing themselves to public disapproval. Their thin ranks were now filled. Finally, they overflowed. The Dreyfus Affair had become a political affair which permitted the Radicals to recapture power and the socialists to slide in behind them. . . .

Brisson, the old man of the left who became President of the Council, already leaned towards revision. A Radical like him, an ardent patriot, sincere in his beliefs, his Minister of War was Godefroy Cavaignac, a great republican name that had been found on the side of civilization in the Panama Affair. If there existed proof of Dreyfus' innocence, if there were traces of irregularity in the trial, Godefroy Cavaignac could be relied on to speak the truth, whatever it was. As a matter of fact, he studied the dossier, became convinced that Dreyfus was guilty, and affirmed it before the Chamber by reading from the tribunal several documents, one of which, coming from the Italian military attaché, Panizzardi, was particularly crushing in its condemnation. The revisionist cause appeared lost at the moment when one had believed it all but won.

That was July 7, 1898. Five weeks later the officer entrusted by the Ministry to the study of the Affair, Captain Cuignet, discovered that the Panizzardi letter was apocryphal. Lt. Colonel Henry, of the Intelligence Office, confessed that he had fabricated it two years after the trial of Dreyfus when the revisionist campaign had begun, in order to display a plain, precise document, an *epitomé* of proof of some sort, which would dispense with any other explanation. He denied that he had, properly speaking, committed a forgery. Arrested on a charge of forgery as his adversary, Colonel Picquart, had been before him, Colonel Henry was led to Mont Valérien where, the following day, August 11, he cut his throat.

The Dreyfus party triumphed. It proclaimed that the innocence of the condemned man was re-established. The new evidence necessary for revision was available and Brisson insisted that it be taken up at once. Cavaignac submitted his resignation, stating his disagreement with the President of the Council and reaffirmed his belief in the guilt of Dreyfus.

It seemed that the Affair, this time, was coming to an end. But the discovery of Henry's forgery, if it shook the public, until then persuaded on the whole that the judgment had been regular, if it threw doubts on the sincerity or on the clairvoyance of the General Staff, it had nothing to do with the trial of 1894 since the apocryphon was posterior to the judgment and thus did not contribute the condemnation. Furthermore, Captain Cuignet, who had discovered the forgery, in giving testimony of his perspicacity and of his good faith, affirmed the authenticity of other documents. One found himself, therefore, once again in a strange situation. The Henry forgery created an immense effect in favor of the thesis of innocence. Its judicial value was null. Neither of the two decrees of revision were to take it into account. The Affair was exasperating. There was no end. . . .

Fear always explains more than one thinks. If the left began to dread the nationalists, the bulk of the Chamber remained moderate and took fright at the Dreyfusard campaign, which, by virtue of its newfound allies, took on a revolutionary character. At the beginning, the party of rehabilitation did not know on whom to rely. The Dreyfus family had first approached the soldiers themselves. Some were found to listen to its complaints, most importantly, Colonel Picquart, but it only aggravated things. It was only natural that with the development of the Affair, those who possessed influence were approached. Joseph Reinach relates how the heads of Catholic organizations were asked for help. The defenders of Dreyfus threatened that in the absence of religious cooperation they would be led to seek assistance from anticlericals and socialists, which might take the Republic away from the *"ralliément."* It became the line of attack: "If I cannot move the gods, I will put all Hades into motion," and was expressed in popular terms by the threat of an "upheaval." If these approaches were made to the Catholics, and it is not unlikely, it is understandable that they were not anxious to enter into one such adventure, to separate themselves from a government which, in the time of Méline, gave them so little cause for complaint that the coming of a "clerical Republic" no longer seemed impossible. In short, to associate the Church in an enterprise which, by the nature of things, was directed against the heads of the Army, would revive the old reproaches of ultra-montanism, and appeared supremely imprudent. The idea could hardly be accepted.

It was easier for the Dreyfus party to enroll radical elements. Those whom Joseph Reinach called "professional agitators," quickly responded. Others, even "less pure," did not hesitate to join them. In fact it was seen that all who had an interest in disorder and in taking revenge espoused the cause of Dreyfus. Socialists entered *en masse* with Jaurès. Clemenceau had preceded them, guided by all his instincts, those of the republican enemy of hierarchy, those of the exile to private life who ached to return to the stage. . . .

. . . Suddenly, on February 16, 1899,

Félix Faure died. The fifth presidency was again interrupted by an accident and the death proved so unfortunate for some, so fortunate for others, that many would not believe it was natural. Félix Faure was notoriously anti-Dreyfusard. . . . Forty-eight hours after his death he was replaced, and Méline, as a candidate, was defeated in advance. The assembly at Versailles preferred Émile Loubet, who after Panama took refuge in senatorial honors, and he was elected by the left although he nourished conservative sentiments. . . .

Paris resented his election and viewed it as an injury and a challenge. The new President entered the Élysée to the cries of "Panama." It was easy to understand that a new era and a new policy had begun. Paul Déroulède tried to oppose it by force. In the afternoon of February 23rd, after Félix Faure's funeral service and counting on the cooperation of the Army and the crowd, he made a romantic attempt at a *coup d'état.* Seizing the bridle of General Roget's horse, at the head of the troops who had attended the funeral, he tried to persuade the general, particularly detested by the Dreyfusards, to march on the Élysée. The latter refused and had Déroulède arrested. The latter was acquitted by a jury three months later.

During the brief adventure the attitude of the soldiers had been perfectly correct. When, a little later, Major Marchand returned to France, he, too, refused to be swayed by public opinion. There was no new Boulanger, but republicans still took alarm and for the very reasons for which nationalists were excited. On June 3 the Court of Cassation ordered the revision of Dreyfus' trial for reasons from which the Henry forgery was excluded. It only specified the communication to the judges of 1894 of a secret document "considered" inapplicable to the condemned, and the attribution of the *bordereau* to "another officer." The same day, Esterhazy, still taking refuge in England, declared himself the true author of the *bordereau* while giving contradictory and even absurd explanations. Without doubt he had written the document, but "on orders," and the real culprit was Dreyfus. However, the latter, removed from detention on Devil's Island, had to appear before a new court-martial at Rennes. . . .

[The Affair] continued to be a source of agitation, and while Waldeck-Rousseau was able to end it, one might say that everything conspired to prolong it. The Rennes court-martial was to render the definitive judgment which both parties necessarily had to accept. A new trial would provide the answers so long sought. Who had committed the act of treason? Dreyfus was accused of it. Esterhazy had said, "I wrote the *bordereau.*" To compare them, to have the two men confront each other appeared to have been the means of resolving the problem because the problem was to choose between two culprits. Esterhazy was cited as witness. Taking refuge in London, he refused to respond to the summons. By what tacit and bizarre agreement did the two parties agree to his absence? The Government proposed to proceed anyway. Demange, Dreyfus' counsel, declared that he had no comments to make and without protests on his part, the court-martial decided that the deposition of Esterhazy was not indispensable to the manifestation of the truth. Thus a man calls himself innocent, asserting that he had not written the famous document of which another declares himself the author. His trial was reopened for reasons the most important of which was the latter's confession, and his own lawyer does not insist on hearing the *confitentem reum* as if the confession were not worthy of being considered, as if it were not legitimate, as if it did not exist. This is what, from afar, appears prodigious to us. It is even more prodigious that people at the time were not struck by it.

From afar it also seems to us that the partisans of innocence were more concerned with having it acknowledged that Dreyfus was not the author of the crime, than with establishing that the crime had

another author. Demange was even content to plead doubt. It is impossible to understand why it was necessary to exonerate Dreyfus and deny the allegations raised against him if it was indisputable that Esterhazy had written the *bordereau,* inasmuch as the guilt of Esterhazy revealed the innocence of Dreyfus.

The man convicted in 1894, however, although personally present, was always "a symbol." The two camps faced each other at Rennes where Dreyfusards and anti-Dreyfusards had thronged, posing generalizations and theses above questions of fact. The witnesses for the prosecution, demonstrating, as in 1894, that the traitor could only be in the artillery, an officer, and probationer on the General Staff, convinced the judges. By five votes to two the court-martial again condemned Dreyfus.

While condemning, however, the military judges wished to appease. They conceded extenuating circumstances and reduced the penalty. Waldeck-Rousseau, who expected an acquittal, was greatly irritated by the verdict. He reacted by granting a pardon. President Loubet signed it at once and Dreyfus accepted it, waiving his right to appeal. One believed it was over. Galliffet gave the order of the day to the Army: "The incident is closed."

It was not an incident. A long time before, the Dreyfus Affair surpassed Dreyfus the individual. It continued when it had ceased to interest the public, Dreyfus himself, and his friends. It was never to finish. The party of the condemned did not disarm. The Affair which had given it power permitted it to keep power and to take reprisals. To maintain the revolutionary agitation which had proven so profitable for the progressive parties, Jaurès sought rehabilitation with the tenacity that already had led to revision. Seven years after the Rennes judgment he obtained a decree of cassation which declared Dreyfus innocent, while still acknowledging that in 1894 a "major crime" had been committed, and without it being legally established that Esterhazy was to blame. The Court had excused the man condemned at Rennes from appearing before a third court-martial only by changing the law and by renouncing its own jurisdiction. If anti-Dreyfusards protested, sincere Dreyfusards groaned, those who wanted the victim rehabilitated one great day, and by the same tribunals which had twice condemned him. The "great crime" which had embroiled France disappeared on the very grounds and considerations that once again proclaimed its existence. One was quite removed from the judicial drama. Several of those who had taken part had already changed camp. It is still being disputed in our day. The decisive revelation awaited from Berlin has not come. The "notebooks" of Schwartzkoppen have been published. Opposing presumptions are still being derived. . . .

III. THE AFFAIR IN PERSPECTIVE

The Thesis of the Two Guilty Parties

FRANÇOIS GOGUEL

François Goguel has combined a distinguished career in history and political science with important government service. He has long taught at the renowned École des Sciences Politiques, helped pioneer research in electoral geography, and held the offices of Director of Service of the Council of the Republic and Secretary General of the Senate. The work from which the following is taken, his *Politique des Partis sous la IIIe République*, is a basic handbook for the study of the period.

THE Dreyfus Affair opened in 1894 and only came to an end, strictly speaking, in 1906. But it was from 1897 to 1900 that it exerted profound influence on French public opinion.

Captain Alfred Dreyfus, an Israelite of Alsatian origin, probationer on the Army General Staff, had been accused of treason at the end of 1894. The basis of the accusation was an unsigned letter which had been removed from the papers of the German military attaché and transmitted to French Intelligence. The letter — to be called the *bordereau* — announced the forwarding of a certain number of secret documents concerned particularly with the artillery. This detail directed suspicion towards Dreyfus whose Jewish religion and rather cold personality had rendered him uncongenial to his colleagues. It was difficult, however, to conceive of the motives for his treason; Dreyfus was rich, led a very orderly life, and came from a family that had left Alsace in 1871 in order to remain French. There no doubt existed some similarities between his handwriting and that of the author of the *bordereau*,

but this was only a very fragile clue and General Mercier, Minister of War, at first hesitated to begin proceedings that risked ending in an acquittal. It appeared that the threat of a campaign which the anti-semitic newspaper, *La Libre Parole*, was prepared to lead against him, helped to overcome his scruples. Captain Dreyfus was arrested and brought before a court-martial in Paris. He strongly protested his innocence, and it is likely that he would have been acquitted had not the Minister of War, without the knowledge of his colleagues in the Dupuy Cabinet, communicated a secret dossier to the judges, prepared by the Second Bureau, unknown to the accused and his lawyers, and which appeared at first sight, overwhelming. On December 22, 1894, Dreyfus was condemned to military degradation and to perpetual deportation in a fortified enclosure.

There was deep and widespread indignation against the "traitor." Jaurès regretted that he had not been shot. Anti-semitic journalists, who helped bring about the decision to prosecute, found in the condemna-

From François Goguel, *La Politique des Partis sous la IIIe République* (Paris, 1946), pp. 86–89, 98–100. Reprinted by permission of the Éditions du Seuil. Translated by the editor.

tion of an Israelite officer a powerful argument to support their theses.

But the convict, transported to Devil's Island, had not confessed. His family believed in his innocence and hoped to succeed in having it acknowledged. His brother, Mathieu, assisted by the writer, Bernard Lazare, led an investigation which could not remain secret; in the first place he addressed himself to the prisoner's superiors of 1894 and asked the officers of the General Staff for a revision of the trial. He approached certain Catholic personalities as well. These steps disturbed the Second Bureau, which then sought to gather new proofs of Dreyfus' guilt and to alert the anti-semitic press.

They loudly exposed the efforts of the Dreyfus family and denounced the formation of a "syndicate" by those who wished to have the traitor declared innocent. There was an interpellation in the Chamber in 1896. The hypothesis of a juridical error was still acceptable, if not probable, given the absence of a confession and the inability of the prosecution to offer a motive for the crime; but such a hypothesis was deemed harmful for the honor of the Army and its chiefs. The defenders of Dreyfus were accused of anti-patriotism, and that impressed many simple souls who were unable to distinguish between an affirmation of innocence and vindication of treason.

However, the new researches of the General Staff, confided to Major Picquart, had an unexpected result; the investigator became convinced that Dreyfus was not guilty. He came into possession of a new document, the *petit-bleu*, stolen from the German embassy. It was a letter written by the military attaché to Major Esterhazy, and then torn and discarded. Picquart was subsequently to be accused of forging this document, but — although prosecuted by his superiors — to be acquitted. The *petit-bleu* directed suspicion to Esterhazy; Picquart undertook an investigation which confirmed it. Of Hungarian origin, "a man lost in debts and deprived of honor," Es-

terhazy used an onionskin paper identical to that of the *bordereau*; his handwriting, more so than that of Dreyfus, resembled that of the *bordereau*, the essential basis of the 1894 trial.

Picquart informed his superiors of his conclusions. But they refused to face a revision of the 1894 trial. In order to explain their attitude some hypotheses must be formulated. It is hardly likely that they had been guided by respect for the rendered judgment, a sentiment proper for jurists, but frequently evoked afterwards. Perhaps they feared the attacks of the anti-semitic press, which, if they had recognized Dreyfus' innocence, would have accused them of having been paid by the "syndicate." I think that an oversimplified conception of discipline and the conviction that an officer discredits himself in acknowledging a mistake, were the major reasons for the attitude of Picquart's superiors. It is also possible that an officer guilty of treason, having kept his post and influence on the General Staff, had sought to prevent any new inquiry to ward off suspicion. In any case, Picquart, previously promoted to Lt. Colonel, was sent to Tunisia, and Esterhazy was declared non-active because of temporary disabilities. But there was no question of reopening the Dreyfus trial.

Picquart thought that he had no right to remain quiet. He communicated the results of his investigation to a friend, the lawyer, Leblois. The latter contacted one of the vice-presidents of the Senate, the senator for life, Scheurer-Kestner, who, like Dreyfus and Picquart himself, was of Alsatian origin. Bernard Lazare and Mathieu Dreyfus had already informed him of the results of the inquiry they had undertaken. Thanks to that twofold source of information, Scheurer-Kestner was in possession of proofs which seemed decisive to him. Counting on personal friends within the Méline Cabinet, he anticipated few difficulties in obtaining revision of the 1894 trial.

But the Government feared that revision would unleash agitation which might prove fatal to it, in arousing the opposition of those Catholics who had supported Drumont's anti-semitic campaign. It judged it wiser to quench the Affair; Méline and his Minister of War, General Billot, claimed that the information brought by Scheurer-Kestner did not constitute the "new evidence" necessary for revision, and therefore rejected his request. Informed of the steps taken by the Vice-President of the Senate, the conservative press intensified its campaign of 1896 against the "syndicate" and the "partisans of the traitor. . . ."

On my part, I think that Captain Alfred Dreyfus was not guilty of the acts of treason for which he was condemned. None of the evidence and presumptions used against him appear conclusive. And many reasons make me judge unlikely the hypothesis of his guilt.

The obscurities of the Affair, however, and its inexplicable elements are still so numerous that I feel able to propose an explanation of it which must remain to a large degree, conjectural. Here is what seems most plausible to me. I think that at the time when the acts were committed which were attributed to Dreyfus, Esterhazy was delivering information to the German military attaché. He was a few years later, but in an ambiguous manner, to confess that he was the author of the *bordereau*, and some physical circumstances render the fact likely. However it is difficult to believe that he was guilty of all the acts of which Dreyfus was accused. This was the principal argument of the anti-revisionists, and it has never been wholly refuted; the "departure for manoeuvres," of which the *bordereau* speaks, corresponds to no known episode in the life of Esterhazy. Moreover, it would appear that the latter was not in a position to obtain the documents mentioned in the *bordereau*.

The *petit-bleu*, however, leaves no doubts as to his guilt. But the latter remains difficult to define as to its precise object.

That is why, to take into account the amazing complexities of the Affair, it is necessary in my opinion, to suppose the existence of two culprits. Such a conjecture appears legitimate in so sinister an affair, which according to Jacques Bainville, "has not yet ceased being disputed, even in our days." The decisive revelation long awaited from Berlin has not come. The notebooks of Schwartzkoppen have been published; opposing presumptions are still being taken from it. Actually, these presumptions all appear to me to favor Dreyfus' innocence, but it is true that Schwartzkoppen has not precisely indicated the name of the guilty party. This is one of the reasons why I think that there had to be one of them who remained unknown.

Does not this hypothesis shed light on things? Two officers, each unknown to the other, furnish documents to the German embassy. One of them is Esterhazy. We are ignorant of the other's identity. Then it becomes clear why, even before the Affair entered its public phase, the General Staff straight-away rejected the request for revision made by the Dreyfus family. One of the culprits remained in the War Office, where he perhaps held an important position. The condemnation of 1894 protected him, and he was dead set on preventing it again being brought into question. He tried, therefore, to "re-enforce" the dossier against Dreyfus and to combat any idea of revision. When Esterhazy began to be mentioned, he must have first thought that once again it was a question of an innocent man, a victim of appearances. But he desired his acquittal because two contrasting judgments based on the same facts would lead to a new inquiry, which risked making the truth known. Then the culprit understood what was happening, and he perceived that Esterhazy was not innocent. He nevertheless insisted on the sole guilt of Dreyfus and opposed reopening the case. It must have been easy for him, in exploiting the attacks against the Army which began to multiply in the revisionist press at the beginning of

1898, to turn the attitude of his superiors in the desired direction.

All this is evidently only a hypothesis; but save the discovery of new documents, I do not think that any degree of certainty can ever be attained. Of all the conceivable explanations, the guilt of Dreyfus, the sole guilt of Esterhazy, and the double guilt of Esterhazy and a third party, is it not the last which best agrees with the established facts while, at the same time, clears up those which remain obscure?

The Affair Without Dreyfus

MARCEL THOMAS

Marcel Thomas, the Conservator of the Bibliothèque Nationale, has written with authority on subjects ranging from the trial of Mary Stuart to the exploits of Roland. In this, the most recent history of the Dreyfus Affair, he minimizes the private motives of the chief protagonists and passes over the personal role of Captain Dreyfus. Making extensive use of newly available archival material, the author stresses instead the structural and psychological aspects of the Case.

THE Dreyfus Affair becomes wholly incomprehensible when removed from the atmosphere of secret warfare in which it steadily developed. Many episodes, moreover (and one suspects not the least enlightening), may be explained by the very special mentality ultimately acquired by those who belong, in no matter what capacity, to the secret services. Officers specializing in the collection of information, or in hunting spies, policemen of all types, secret agents, doubles or triples, blackmailers and forgers, too (entirely necessary when it was a matter of "intoxicating" the enemy); such were the veritable overseers in the thoroughly secret part of the Dreyfus Affair, of which the public and even the often abused government, usually had only illusory glimpses.

It is these secrets, big and small, of our intelligence service, that we are going to try to illuminate. To the degree that they are related to the development of the Dreyfus Affair, it will be seen, we think, that they have greatly influenced its course.

As important as they are, however, the activities of Intelligence do not suffice to explain everything. Even after giving them their just place, one must still ask himself why so many high-ranking or general officers, well-situated by their duties to know the truth, in fact showed themselves incapable of understanding it, diluted and fragmented as it was among so many different departments and offices so that no one managed any longer to grasp it in its entirety. Even if acknowledged that some members of the General Staff had sometimes obeyed petty prejudices, even base personal motives, it would still not be admissible for so many to have yielded to the temptation of a hasty Manicheism, something which could not be imagined today. To range without hesitation all the partisans of revision on the side of the good angels and all its adversaries on the side of the devils, was no doubt excusable in the heat of action, when it was necessary at any price to sway public opinion. Today, on the other hand, we ought less to judge than to understand. To assume, with fifty years of perspective, that all the crack officers concerned with the Affair were without exception fools or scoundrels, would be as much an injustice as an absurdity.

Appearances can sometimes be deceiving; it would be advisable, therefore, in order not to fall into any trap, to examine very closely the role played by each of the wheels of the heavy machine between which an innocent man found himself crushed. Such a study could not be undertaken by the Court of Cassation, except in

From Marcel Thomas, *L'Affaire sans Dreyfus* (Paris, 1961), pp. 10–11, 13, 71–72, 104–05, 108–11, 113–15, 119, 130–31, 134–35, 140–41, 158–59, 278. Reprinted by permission of the Librairie Arthème Fayard. Translated by the editor.

41

an indirect way, because its task was only to establish the innocence or guilt of Dreyfus, not to determine the administrative and moral responsibility incurred by a Mercier, a Sandherr, a Gonse, or a Henry. . . .

One sees, therefore, that the title, somewhat surprising perhaps, is not unjustified. As a matter of fact, Dreyfus, as an individual, fills only a very small space in this book consecrated to the Affair which bears his name. This is not the result of a deliberate attempt to minimize the physical and mental suffering necessarily endured by the unfortunate officer, a victim both of calamity, prejudice, and blindness, and the cowardice of those who, with a peaceful conscience, would send him to prison and do everything possible to prevent him from ever returning. If we have had to pass very quickly over the parts of the drama which touch directly on the person of Dreyfus, it is that everything has already been said about it, and that after the publication of the martyr's letters and memoirs, nothing could decently be added. On the very substance of the Affair, Dreyfus, until 1899, was assuredly the least informed man in the world and therein, moreover, lies not the least tragic and paradoxical aspect of his unhappy fate.

We have not sought (it was soon obvious there was no space) to refute one by one the thousand legends which have haunted the Affair and whose ashes are still rekindled in new forms. Nevertheless, because the posthumous journal of Paléologue gave new life to certain rumors which were already circulating by 1906, we have, in an appendix, studied the legend of the "third man" in the light of contemporary documents, at the same time that we try to show why the thesis (belatedly asserted by Esterhazy), according to which the real author of the *bordereau* would have been a hidden agent of our Intelligence Service, or Mercier himself, encounters almost insurmountable obstacles. . . .

The Intelligence Service. A "home-like" atmosphere, on the other hand, prevailed within the Department. That certainly did not prevent jealousies or squabbles, but against the outside the Department at once presented a solid front. The importance attributed to their duties by this little nucleus of officers was no doubt excessive, but they were sincerely convinced of it, and their *esprit de corps* engendered in them a strong mistrust of the other departments — above all, those which had the misfortune to be confided to civilians. They considered themselves above all suspicion, alone capable of efficiently guarding state secrets. It is hardly an exaggeration to say that the Statistical Section to a certain degree considered itself superior to all the established powers — including the government and ministers, whose discretion, patriotism, and integrity it did not hesitate to survey and to evaluate secretly.

This state of mind, quite usual in higher echelons of the police departments of the world, explains many aspects of the Affair. The chief of the Section, who managed its affairs by himself, alone knew all its personnel and sources of information, which he avoided revealing as much as possible, even to his superiors on the General Staff. He considered himself personally bound to his sources and compelled to keep them a professional secret from all third parties. From the day that the results obtained began to justify the confidence placed in him, he did not feel obliged to account to anyone. We will see that Lt. Colonel · Picquart, when he succeeded Sandherr in 1895, quickly attuned himself to this very contagious state of mind. . . .

On the arrival of the BORDEREAU. The circumstances in which the Statistical Section came into possession of the letter sent by Esterhazy to Schwartzkoppen at the end of August have long appeared to constitute one of the most impenetrable mysteries of the Dreyfus Affair. Few episodes, however, can be described as easily, and above all, in a way so consistent with the official version given by the General Staff.

Actually, that pseudo-enigma derived from the quite excusable optical illusion to which all those succumbed who, in the course of the struggles for revision, were anxiously questioned about the wanderings of the famous document. In fact, from 1894 until the Zola trial, that is, for over four years, the manner by which it was acquired had been dissimilated with care by the military authorities, for obvious reasons of security and diplomatic propriety. When, quite reluctantly, they decided to reveal the truth, so much ink had already been spilled about the Affair, so many hypotheses had been advanced, the document itself had been subjected to so many analyses, valuations, and re-evaluations of all types that no one could succeed any longer in representing those two small sheets of onionskin paper under the very banal aspect presented in September, 1894, when Henry and Sandherr saw it for the first time. For them it was originally an espionage document, certainly interesting, even alarming, but comparable to those which passed through their hands every day. . . .

It appears certain that the *bordereau,* written a month earlier by Esterhazy, was found in the group of papers delivered to Henry by Mme. Bastian. Contrary to what was too often affirmed or allowed to be understood, the *bordereau* did not come alone to the Statistical Section. It was, on the contrary, part of a rather copious delivery, including at least half a dozen interesting documents, submerged as usual in trifles. This point of fact is significant because it permits the replacement of the episode in its true context, that is, in the banal routine of the "usual route." The General Staff, it is true, had long concealed the fact that the *bordereau* had not come as an isolated document; it wished to keep as secret as possible the activities of Mme. Bastian. . . .

At the time that Reinach conceived [his] hypothesis, he had just been made aware, by the testimony of Major Cordier, of the existence of the agent Brücker and the re-

lationship of the Millescamp Affair to the Dreyfus Affair. He knew on the other hand that Schwartzkoppen claimed never to have seen the *bordereau.* His imagination did the rest, and the legend of the agent Brücker was presented by him in the press and then in his book with such strength and talent that it quickly became intangible dogma for most revisionists. And yet, on closer observation, the facts render it untenable.

First let us notice that the "disgrace" of Brücker only existed in Reinach's mind. After the Millescamp Affair, Brücker continued to serve the Statistical Section with the same regularity as in the past, at least until 1899. At most he was occupied elsewhere and in a different way, when Reinach insisted that he was henceforward "burned" at the embassy. He therefore had no reason to "seek pardon" from his chiefs. Furthermore, there is in every way a glaring improbability in ascribing to him a particularly audacious *coup d'éclat* which would have taken place in the very embassy in connection with which his former mistress had denounced him. . . .

Reinach was certainly aware of the major failure in his argument. Persuaded that Henry was an accomplice to Esterhazy's treason, he was unable to explain why, in these conditions, the *bordereau* had not been destroyed at the moment of its arrival by the one who could have been so inconvenienced by it. After all, the error which was fatal to Dreyfus need not have been committed. We will even see that it almost failed to have occurred. Hence, for the historian, the necessity of an explanation which he believed he had found in the alleged threat of blackmail he attributed to Brücker.

Once freed from this wholly uncalled for hypothesis, we are compelled to state that if Henry did not destroy the *bordereau* as soon as Mme. Bastian delivered it to him, it is because actually the document did not at all worry him and for the excellent reason that Henry was not then the accomplice of Esterhazy. Let us also observe that

Lt. Colonel Picquart, well situated by virtue of his duties from 1895 to 1896, to break through the mysteries of the Statistical Section, always refused to believe in the hypothesis of Henry's complicity. . . .

Certainly Henry might have been unable to recognize Esterhazy's handwriting — and in that case there would not have been a Dreyfus Affair — but he also could not have been able to, and that is what happened. All historic events thus fringe on a greater or smaller zone of indetermination, and it always depends on the thousand imponderables that are brought forth. If the visual memory of Henry had been better . . . If d'Aboville had not been named deputy-chief of the 4th Bureau . . . If Cleopatra's nose . . .

There still remain the assertions of Schwartzkoppen, repeated in the posthumous "Notebooks," according to which he had never seen the *bordereau*. It excludes, for his part, the possibility of the *bordereau* coming to the Ministry by the "usual route," and attributes its delivery to other means, vague and "untidy." At first glance Schwartzkoppen appears a disinterested witness and worthy of being believed. But then . . .

His version was that the *bordereau* had been stolen from the embassy at the time of its arrival there. Since we have established that it was only delivered to Henry, in one way or another, at the end of September, one falls into the difficulties already mentioned. Why did the unknown spy to whom Schwartzkoppen attributed the theft of the document wait so long before delivering it to his superiors? Is it not an amazing coincidence as well that he delivered it at precisely the time Henry reestablished contact with Mme. Bastian? And where did the tears on the *bordereau* come from? What happened to the envelope? Such objections can be multiplied to infinity. . . .

Schwartzkoppen's denials are really a little too frequent: he never discarded the *bordereau* in 1894, he never discarded the *petit-bleu* in 1896, he never even discarded important papers into his wastebasket, "knowing too well where they went." By wishing to convince us of it, he provokes our incredulity, and the bulk of his assertions becomes more than suspect. Must we not attribute them to the vanity of a Prussian Junker, retrospectively vexed at having been the dupe of an illiterate maid for so long, while he prided himself on being an agent of great intelligence? When one is colonel of an élite regiment, patronized and esteemed by William II himself, it is hardly amusing, let us admit, to have to confess that one compromised his ambassador, cast doubts on the word of his emperor, allowed an innocent man to be condemned, and upset an entire country for years, only because, while carrying out his profession of spying, he had neglected to take the most elementary precautions!

It suffices to attribute to Schwartzkoppen a venial lie on this point — a lie, after all, inspired by very understandable motives — in order to dispel all the mysteries which apparently surrounded the coming of the *bordereau* to the Statistical Section. Between his word and the many clues which make us doubt it, how can we hesitate? . . .

The Mechanism of the Error. It is noticeable that, during this first phase of the Affair, a certain haziness long prevailed, particularly about the chronology of events. In the course of the various legal entreaties which evoked, beginning in 1897, the first inquiries made by the Ministry about the time of the *bordereau's* arrival, staff officers tended to move back the date as much as possible, intentionally or not. Some spoke of the end of September, without otherwise specifying, and General Gonse even indicated September 20, forgetting that Henry was then away from Paris. The haste, the confusion which marked the first inquiries were evidently somewhat embarrassing, and everyone, ex-ministers very much included, preferred to be prudently vague. The chronic disorder of the Statistical Section, the deplorable negligence brought forth (due to insufficient personnel, affirmed those responsible, using an argument popular in all the administrations of the world) in dating the documents as they arrived had in no little way contributed to muddle things. . . .

Mercier certainly shared the first conviction of Sandherr and Matton, that the *bordereau* was written by an officer in the Ministry. The enemy was close-by, it had to be relatively easy to unearth him, and Mercier gave strict orders in this sense.

Therein — we know that much today — lay the first error, and with respect to method, the most serious, because all the others followed from it. . . .

The Discovery of the Traitor. Of course it occurred to no one, October 6, 1894, to consider Dreyfus guilty because he was a Jew, but because he was a Jew, the idea of his guilt was accepted, more easily than it would have been for another. Few, in short, were surprised. A man as lucid as Picquart was not the last to allow himself to succumb to this epidemic reflex.

Sandherr, also very anti-semitic, on hearing the name of the suspect cried, "I should never have doubted it." The fact that he was not without doubt until then is especially worthy of being underlined. His assistant, Cordier, who detested Jews, would also say, some days later, "I was far-sighted enough not to have wanted him in my service." The two remarks demonstrated that one had not previously had any reason to suspect Dreyfus, and also that one was confusedly inclined to admit that an Alsatian Jew had more opportunities to betray his country than an Alsatian who was not one.

If chance determined that Esterhazy's writing had not resembled that of Dreyfus, but that of another probationer, one may rest assured that the latter would have been observed more closely, with multiple surveys and investigations. In the case of Dreyfus one went quickly — too quickly — because a subconscious prejudice characterized from its origin the minds of the investigators. Therein lies all the drama. The anti-semitic reflex operating at a bad moment, in delicate circumstances, was sufficient to tip the balance to the wrong side. Not the only reason, but as part of a system of very complex forces, it contributed to forming the resultant which would inevitably draw the heavy ministerial machine in the direction of the error, rapidly becoming irreparable. . . .

The Crime of the Secret Dossier. Mercier decided to prosecute. He certainly cannot be blamed for that first decision, which he took, we think, in good faith and conscience and after having deeply reflected on it. At most, one has the right to state afterwards that it was not judicious. It did not, in any case, in any way taint his honor. Brought by his duties to a case of spying which, whatever the cause, was most serious, he had the right, and no doubt the duty, to at least proceed to a regular inquiry. But a logical chain of circumstances which he doubtless had not anticipated soon led him to understand that this first step once taken, in appearance so harmless, he would no longer be able to reverse the process without compromising his own ministerial career. From the moment when Mercier clearly saw the dilemma, when he would have to choose between the loss of his portfolio and the condemnation of Dreyfus, he would bend, or have bent, the course of events towards a solution that he believed perhaps conformable to justice, if not to legality, but which in any case did not compromise his personal interests. In all truth, Mercier, too, was convinced by Boisdeffre's first report of the guilt of Dreyfus. . . .

Because of his activities, the Minister of Foreign Affairs was much more apt than Mercier to appreciate the dangerous consequences that the proceedings against Drey-

fus risked having in the diplomatic sphere
— consequences which his colleague did
not even seem to have considered. Hanotaux forcefully declared that if Dreyfus
were a hundred times guilty, it was in his
opinion impossible to reveal information
based on a document irregularly taken
from a foreign embassy in defiance of extra-
territorial rights, and which, moreover,
jeopardized duly accredited diplomatic representatives. The *bordereau,* in fact, had a
criminal character only to the degree it was
sent to a foreign military attaché. To declare publicly that Schwartzkoppen carried
on espionage would provoke sufficient complications (the precedent of the Borup affair demonstrated it well enough), but to
avow that our secret services burgled em-
bassies would thoroughly put us in the
wrong and would produce completely justi-
fied German protests. Hanotaux, therefore,
declared himself opposed to proceedings
taken on such bases and even against the
principle of any continuation of the inquiry. . . .

Mercier in any case held fast and un-
fortunately succeeded in persuading the
President of the Council of his views. By
one of those bad compromises so frequently
made in such a case, Dupuy had him
promise, however, on the insistence of
Hanotaux, that if no other proofs than the
bordereau were discovered against the suspected officer, the proceedings would be
abandoned. It was a promise weighty with
consequences for the unfortunate Dreyfus,
because it marked the origin of the "secret
dossier" that would be dragged to the
second revision like a heavier and heavier
chain. In fact, when one month later, the
investigation had not discovered the shadow
of a new proof, Mercier would not hesitate
to have it sought and found — actually,
forged — by the Statistical Section. . . .

Sandherr and his subordinates lost no
time. Their involvement having begun
with the mention of the name Dreyfus, it
led in November to the creation of a first
secret dossier, the embryo of the enormous

heap of true and false documents to be
waded through, beginning in 1898, by revisionists and anti-revisionists. The work
carried out by the Section happily left
traces so one can re-create their method
today without fear of major error. Once
released, the wheels of the diabolical
mechanism fitted up against Dreyfus began to turn. One better understands why
the 1894 trial was later viewed by the
General Staff as an intangible work of our
counter-espionage service which would
have been disorganized, to the great cost
of national security, if its methods of work
had been divulged. One can also appreciate, we believe, the motives which im-
pelled the collaborators of Sandherr and
Henry, in the highest ranks, to defend ob-
stinately and by less and less admissible
conduct, the operation organized by them
in common and by their former chief. . . .

The error, the crime committed two
years before by Mercier and his subordinates, prevented the latter from simply de-
claring that they made a mistake and now
asked only to correct their error. It was
because the trial of 1894 had been poorly
conducted, because the sentence rendered
had been not only iniquitous but fraudulent, that it was unable to be corrected. It
was a paradoxical, vicious circle which
would be the end of the one who managed
to break it.

One certainly has the right to charge
atrocious cowardice to these men who, in
order to avoid a scandal ("the mire," said
Gonse), accepted, no doubt more light-
heartedly than claimed, the martyrdom of
an innocent man. But to be just, in their
case too, it must not be forgotten that his
innocence was not believed in, could not
be believed in, and would not be believed
in completely. The position of a Gonse, or
a Boisdeffre, or of a Billot was above all
opportunistic. Whether one blames or
praises them, there always have been, there
will always be, men — and not insignificant ones — who prefer injustice to dis-

order. It is essentially a question of temperament. Such options, however, require at
least a minimum of lucidity and an exact
appreciation of the forces involved. In the
circumstances, the decision of Gonse,
warmly approved by his superiors, unfor-
tunately could only create disorder and
perpetuate injustice.

The Affair as Accident and Error

GUY CHAPMAN

Guy Chapman, formerly Professor of Modern History at the University of
Leeds, has just published a history of the Third Republic. The selections which
follow are taken from his book on the Dreyfus Affair and show a strongly
revisionist approach. Chapman spurns the notion of conspiracy and almost
eliminates the role usually attributed to anti-semitism. The General Staff, he
insists, was guilty only of genuine error and mistaken loyalty.

For some years I have been engaged
on a study of the French Third Republic. As everyone knows who reads the
history of France between 1870 and 1914,
the Dreyfus case lies in his way, a vast
and distracting maze, *una selva oscura*. It
cannot be avoided. Unhappily much legend is attached to the Affair. To accept the
conventional reading of a clerico-military
conspiracy is to swallow the propaganda of
the Dreyfusards. No conspiracy existed in
military circles, none in clerical. The arrest
of Déroulède and his allies in August,
1899, was no more than the spectacular
method of a shaky and nervous Government of rallying opinion to its side. This
consideration led me back to a re-examina-
tion of the evidence from the beginning.
It soon became apparent that much more is
to be said for the War Office than has generally been admitted, that anti-semitism
played little, perhaps no, part in the arrest
of the unhappy victim or in his trial, that
the accusations against the secular Church
and, save the Assumptionists, against the
religious Orders have the flimsiest foundations. In short, the conventional story is
overlaid with propaganda put out by partisans on both sides.

To explain all this would occupy far
more space than could be spared in a history covering seventy years. I therefore decided to treat this fragment in isolation and
at greater length than I could in the context of the history of France. I have here
dealt with nothing but the case and the
internal politics connected with it. I have
omitted everything touching foreign affairs
save as they impinge on the case. I have
omitted all questions of economics, finance,
labour, and so forth. I have sketched in,
far more roughly than I hope to do later,
the necessary background of party politics,
the Army and the Church, and the changes
wrought by the case. . . .

In spite of the overwhelming and rapid
defeat of 1870, the Army remained both
popular and respected. There was its long
and glorious tradition from the days when
it was said that no war could occur without
the presence of the French, through the
great period when the armies of the First
Republic had overrun Europe — "O
Soldats de l'An II! O guerres! O épopées!"
— through the Napoleonic epoch, the Algerian conquest, the Crimea, Magenta and
Solferino and finally, even in defeat, the
memories of Mars-la-Tour and Patay. And
there was the fact that at least two men in
three had served in its ranks for three years
and upwards, not only plebeians but also
bourgeois and aristocrats. Few Frenchmen
doubted that in the rooms of the War
Office in the Rue Saint-Dominique the staff

From *The Dreyfus Case*, Reynal and Company, Inc., pp. 9, 37–41, 62–66, 357–360. Copyright,
1955, by Guy Chapman. Reprinted by permission of Brandt & Brandt.

of the "silent service," *le grand silencieux,* were preparing the plans which in one invincible sweep would drive the Germans from the lost provinces.

On the other hand, the politicians of the Republic were torn between the popular sentiment, which as Frenchmen they shared, and the distrust they felt as Republicans. Republican histories showed a professional army which had supported Charles X in 1830, had shot down the workers in June, 1848, had gone over to Louis Napoleon in 1851 against the Second Republic, and had massacred the Communards of Paris in 1871. They believed the Army to be a political instrument; they were wrong in their reading. The history of the Army shows it to have been nonpolitical. Every time it had been drawn into civil crises, the officers had done no more than obey the orders of their highest authority, the Minister of War. That was why in 1851 Louis Napoleon on the eve of the *coup d'état* had placed at the head of the War Office the single General on whom he could rely, Saint-Arnaud, "an obscure brigadier-general, whose *condottiere* spirit was unembarrassed by scruples." He knew that the War Minister would be obeyed.

For their suspicions the Republicans had themselves to thank. The legislature of 1877–81 had insisted on the purge of the non-Republican elements in the civil service, and had given the vacant places to their friends and parasites. That of 1881–85 did much the same with the judiciary. It had not become impossible, but it was certainly difficult, for a member of a Royalist family to enter the civil service. "Former pupil of the Jesuits, former abjuring member of a Republican committee, former active, though nonetheless sceptical, member of a Boulangist committee, my unworthiness seemed solidly established. And how heavily charged my ancestry: a great-grandfather shot at Quiberon and a great-grand-uncle dead in the September massacres." Thus M. de Saint-Aulaire on his

attempts to sit — only to sit — the examinations for the Foreign Office.

The single institution on which the Republicans had not laid their sacrilegious hands was the Army. For one thing, as in all armies in the late nineteenth century, the pay was abominable, while, with continuing peace, promotion was slow. It was thus not a career for the ambitious, but it could be one for those to whom the other departments of State were closed. Therefore the professional officers who had entered through Saint-Cyr tended to be drawn from what in England would be called the county families. Many Saint-Cyriens came from homes untouched by the ideas of the Great Revolution. It is noteworthy that after the Revolution of 1830, and again after the *coup d'état* of 1851, the sons of many famous military families no longer entered the Army, refusing to serve the usurpers. It was only after 1870 that they reappeared, possibly to some extent influenced by the decline in income from rents caused by the agricultural slump at the end of the seventies.

Most of these officers had been educated in Catholic, not in State schools, but this no more implies that they were devout than an education at Westminster or Winchester implies that an English boy is a classicist and a royalist. They were believing but not necessarily practising Catholics. Interested publicists were later to take up the theme that the General Staff was Jesuit-trained and controlled: but as the Comte de Mun wrote in *The Times* (17 January 1899), "Of the hundred and eighty officers who last year composed the General Staff, there were hardly as many as nine or ten belonging to that category." Major Ducassé, giving evidence at the final revision of the Dreyfus case, said: "They say I acted under the orders of Father du Lac. Odd. I was not at a Jesuit school, but at a lay one. Though I am in fact a Catholic born, I am a free-thinker. I am so little clerical that I married a Protestant. Since the formalities of the Church are irksome, I married in a Protestant *temple.* I have one daughter,

and she's a Protestant. That's how clerical
I am."

It remains true that the officers were almost all nominal Catholics. The infantry
and cavalry were less exposed to alien influences than the artillery and engineer
officers, who had passed through the Poly-
technic and rubbed shoulders with civilians
and Republicans, and, generally speaking,
did not reach the highest commands. In
spite of the fact that a number of men well
known to be Republicans did in fact reach
the highest rank in the Army — Divisional
General — it would be true to say that, as
a whole, the officer class, particularly in the
highest ranks, was at best neutral towards
the regime. A convinced Republican officer
was an anomaly. Almost alone, General
Galliffet, whose birth, gallantry, and com-
petence were undeniable, made no bones
about his loyalty to the Republic; but
Galliffet was notoriously eccentric.

The technical cause of this state of affairs
was the system of promotion. This was
regulated by Soult's Law of 1832, by
which, up to the rank of Commandant
(Major), two-thirds of the vacancies were
filled through seniority, but above that
rank half the promotions were by selection
carried out by the Classification Commission of the corps commanders under the
authority of the Minister of War. The
Minister up to 1888 was invariably himself
a general, hence no difficulties arose. From
1888 to 1893 the Ministry was occupied by
de Freycinet, a civilian who to all intents
abdicated from his control over the senior
appointments. Gradually and very naturally, the classification commission tended
to select men of their own way of thinking.
Thus, by the nineties, the successive
changes in the upper hierarchy had produced on the whole a group of conservative
senior officers, in which the Republicans
were a tiny minority. At the height of the
controversy over the Dreyfus case and after,
the politicos and press of the Left were to
talk of a "clerico-military plot"; but the
situation had a simpler and far more realistic cause, merely that like calls to like,

and men elect to their clubs men of their
own kind. In spite of the legends, clericalism played a minimal part in the promotions. . . .

Yet in spite of its prejudices, the Army
was, it must be emphasized, not a political
body. As Pimodan wrote: "In spite of
what has since been claimed, we in the
Army did not go in for politics": he adds
that the half-yearly reports required statements on an officer's morality, education,
and behaviour, but not on his politics or religion. The duty of the Army officer was to
obey his superior officer in all circumstances, however repugnant might be the
task, and whoever might be his commander.
There had in fact been few anti-Republican
demonstrations, even at the height of the
sixteenth of May crisis of 1877. Nothing
could be found against generals known to
be of Royalist or Bonapartist sympathies;
they were simply put on the retired list
because they were suspected. In the late
eighties Boulanger received no backing
from the Army; he was considered an un-
disciplined officer, as well as an upstart.
The automatic resistance to a summons to
act politically will be seen in General
Roget's behaviour after Félix Faure's funeral in February, 1899. The Army regarded itself as sacred, a thing apart and,
as Girardet says, an officer who frequented
civilian circles often had this noted on his
half-yearly report as a bad mark, while
those who advertised their Republicanism
were frowned on for playing politics. . . .

Did the Left at any time believe that the
danger existed? It is difficult to be definite.
Undoubtedly cooler men of great political
experience entertained the idea. Paul Cam-
bon, looking at the attitude of the soldiers
to revision, thought that a revival of
Boulangism might occur: "It may be a general will be found to take up a spectacular
defence of the honour of the Army. But,"
he added, "it is true, I don't see the general." In fact there was none. All the
soldiers desired was to be master in their
own house, without interference from the
politicians, to whip their own dogs, and for

that they were ready to go to lengths, but not to extremes, not to revolt. As isolated as monks from the main currents of civilian society, the generals did not know enough to decline the help of political charlatans who hoped to use them for their own purposes.

Thus there was mutual misunderstanding. The civilians, the Senators and Deputies, were no less ignorant of the Army. They did not attack them on the score of incompetence: they accused them of the one thing from which every general would have drawn back in horror, rebellion. The members of the Army committees in the Chamber and Senate did not know their business, and they permitted freedom to their fellows to attack, on political grounds and for electoral purposes, the institution they should have protected.

There were even weaker foundations for the attacks on the Church. Anti-clerical writers presented the Church as a reactionary body allied to the Army in conspiracy against the Republic. The evidence is thin. In every organisation there are those who cannot be silent. The utterances of a few priests and laymen were identified as the attitude of the whole Church. A sermon of Father Didon, an article by Drumont, would be publicised: the protests of the Abbés Frémont and Brugerette or the Catholic *Salut Public* of Lyon would not be quoted by the anti-clerical press. The Society of Jesus with its romantic reputation for conspiracy was naturally singled out for special treatment, and the confessor of Boisdeffre and de Mun, Father Du Lac, at worst a minor intriguer, pointed to as the centre of the conspiracy. But the Society at this date was far from belligerent. One foolish anti-semitic article in the *Civiltà Cattolica* in January, 1898, does not make a campaign. Father Lecanuet believed it to be an unwise opening shot. Sorel, the anti-clerical, thought it a counter-attack. It may have been either, but what Reinach, for whom it is the basis of his charge of Jesuit anti-semitism, ignored, is a no less violent polemic against the Church

in the *Univers Israélite* published a few days earlier.

The single body which justifies the charges of anti-clerical writers was the Assumptionist Order, plebeian and violent, which did much harm to Vatican policy; which was deplored by many bishops; and over which they had no control. For the Vatican, Dreyfus was a minor matter, of the smallest importance in comparison with the doctrinal warfare which raged during these years throughout the whole Catholic Church. It may well be that, as Monsignor d'Hulst, Rector of the Catholic Institute in Paris and deputy for Brest, said, Rome was blind: but in fact the Biblical controversy was shaking the very foundations of belief, and in such a situation the Dreyfus question agitating Parisian society was of little moment. . . .

The suspected man, Captain Alfred Dreyfus, came from a Jewish family long established in Alsace, that debatable land which the Germans had annexed in 1871. Under the Treaty of Frankfurt-am-Main, French nationals could, within eighteen months of the ratification of the treaty, choose the country to which they would owe allegiance, but those who preferred to remain French citizens must cross the new frontier. The Dreyfus family owned a cotton-spinning mill at Mulhouse. Like many Alsatians and Lorrainers, whether Jew or Gentile, they were passionately French, and like many Jewish families of long residence they were, bating their religion, more French than Jewish, completely assimilated. There were four Dreyfus brothers — Jacques, Mathieu, Alfred, and Léon — and three sisters. In 1871 the whole family opted for French citizenship, except Jacques and Mathieu, who remained in Mulhouse to direct the factory: in 1897 Jacques moved part of the factory over the frontier into the Territory of Belfort.

Alfred Dreyfus had been born on 19 October 1859. In 1882 he had entered the École Polytechnique and later had been commissioned in the artillery. Throughout his career, until he reached the War Office, the reports of his commanding officers had been uniformly excellent; their single unfavourable comment had been the tonelessness of his voice. He had entered the École Supérieure at the end of 1890, sixty-seventh in the list, and had passed out nineteenth. He was then, in January, 1893, seconded as a staff learner to the War Office. In 1890 he had married Lucie Hadamard, the daughter of a Paris diamond merchant, by whom he had two children. Some years earlier he had had a liaison with a young married woman, which he had broken off in response to an appeal by her parents. Beyond this, it seems, he had two brief liaisons of no serious character in 1893 and 1894. Moreover, he was rich. At this date he had a private income of twenty-five to thirty thousand francs and could look forward to inheriting at least fifty thousand francs a year. Everything in his existence cried out against the probability of his being in the pay of Germany.

At the War Office he had passed his first six months in the First Bureau, his second in the Fourth, his third in the Second, and at this date he was attached to the Third. During the staff ride in June, with the other officers he had dined in Boisdeffre's mess on the last evening. Something having arisen about the new guns, Dreyfus described some recent trials at Bourges and Calais so effectively that Boisdeffre after dinner spent an hour walking up and down the Moselle bridge at Charmes in conversation with him. Dreyfus believed that he made a friend of the Chief of Staff. As has been seen, his report from the Fourth Bureau stated that he was unsuited to staff employment. The report from the First Bureau, while stressing his intelligence and width of knowledge, ended: "Desires to and should succeed." From the Second Bureau (Intelligence) Colonel de Sancy, while praising his intellect and adaptability to the work, thought him possibly a little too sure of himself. In this Bureau, however, Sandherr had specially requested that he should not be attached to the Statistical Section. The report from the Third Bureau was not due until December, but Major Picquart, ordered to post the staff learners, had not put him in the Operations Section dealing with secret and confidential matters, but in that of manœuvres.

Generally, it emerges from the testimony given by his brother-officers that Dreyfus was not liked. He was admitted to have an excellent brain, but he was inclined to boast. "I thought his manners" wrote Pimodan, a contemporary in the Rue Saint-Dominique, "not very agreeable, and altogether hardly suited to our society, although I attached no importance to it." Other officers with whom he served said he put his nose into matters which did not concern him, especially mobilisation plans, and talked about them too much. It certainly appears that Dreyfus had an extremely limited range of interests. He was ambitious and a passionate student of military affairs. He seems to have had few interests outside his family; neither literature, music, art nor sport made any appeal. His *Lettres d'un Innocent,* written from his confinement on The Devil's Island, even allowing for the exigencies of censorship, show a man of commonplace, even narrow imagination. It would seem that Dreyfus, with his ambition and self-sufficiency, possessed a simple vanity which made him show off his professional knowledge; this was in itself harmless, but, since talking shop was regarded with disfavour in the Army, it was enough to chill less ambitious men. G. W. Steevens, the English journalist who covered the Rennes trial for the *Daily Mail,* considered he had been "bumptious." Thus when those who had served with him were asked to give evidence, they recalled these trifles, which, in their cumulation, weighed with the judges.

Moreover, one officer (Duchâtelet, at the second trial at Rennes), to whom Dreyfus had been attached for a short time, stated on oath that the accused man had suggested that they should call on a *poule de luxe,* in whose house he said he had lost a large sum of money. Another (Lemonnier, also at Rennes) testified that Dreyfus had boasted to him of being present at German army manœuvres in Alsace. Dreyfus denied the fact of both these things, but Jean France, a Sûreté agent present at the Rennes trial, was certain that both officers were speaking the truth, insofar that Dreyfus had made the statements. This somewhat foolish boasting by a young man, of things he had not done, took its revenge. Dreyfus was vain. He liked to display his capacity, his wide knowledge of secret or confidential topics. He talked ostentatiously of his wealth, perhaps of women. At Rennes an officer, Maistre, compared him with another, Captain Junck, "a very unpretentious lad, very sound, who is counted one of our best. He has a family to support and a sister to coach for her degree. Obviously, compared with him, Dreyfus was on velvet."

Reinach put this hostile evidence down to anti-semitism: that, in fact, is the theme of his history. But, save for Sandherr, who is known to have been a passionate anti-semite, there is no evidence to support this thesis. Anti-semitism no doubt existed, but it cannot be shown to have played a dominant part in the arrest and trial of Dreyfus. As General Lebelin de Dionne, Commandant of the École de Guerre when Dreyfus was a student, said at the Rennes trial, he did not wish the school to be a place of religious persecution, and a Christian would be sent back to his regiment for faults which in a Jew were passed over. So far as the War Office was concerned, apart from Sandherr the only two identifiable anti-semites were Major Picquart of the Third Bureau and Major Cordier of the Statistical Section, both of whom were to struggle on behalf of Dreyfus. Picquart said that anti-semitism was rife in the War Office and that in consequence he had taken care to put Dreyfus in a section where he would have an unprejudiced chief, Lt-Col. Mercier-Milon, and also would not have to deal with security matters. On the other hand, Leblois, himself as deeply involved in the case as Picquart,

remarks: "The case appears essentially to have been an army mistake. . . . We doubt that anti-semitism should be made responsible for the opening of the case, though it seems likely that, at the War Office, an appeal was made to it from the beginning, and it is certain that the case then at once found powerful reinforcement." Again, Bertin-Mourot, the son of a Jewish mother, who wished, Reinach asserts on no evidence, to have this racial stain forgiven, strenuously resisted the accusation that he had desired to get rid of this Jew: "During my time at the War Office the question [anti-semitism] never existed. I cannot give a better proof than that Captain Dreyfus, a learner, was put to work on the most important, the most secret, railway network. From the moment Dreyfus came to us, he was a comrade to whom I handed all my work, all my secrets, the secrets of all my files." Similarly, Aboville, primarily responsible for pitching on Dreyfus, shows not a touch of anti-semitism in his evidence. Reinach says that the whole General Staff, because Dreyfus was a Jew, "was astounded that they had not earlier smelt the Judas," but in that case, how was it that rather more officers gave evidence as to character in Dreyfus's favour than gave evidence against him?

What it is important to recognise is that Dreyfus was accused of the cardinal sin against the Army and the country. The officers were asked to testify to facts and character, and it was their duty to give such evidence as they possessed. The anti-semitic shadow over the case came, not from the Army, but from the press. . . .

Many theories have been propounded, many generalisations presented, as to the meaning of the Affair, usually with a moral tang. Few deserve to survive. The more the evidence is examined, the less heroic and the less odious do the leading actors become. The case was not a battle between good and evil, and such a view simplifies it to meaninglessness.

It passed through three phases. The first concerns only the soldiers and the scattered handful of early revisionists — the victim's family; Reinach and Lazare, alarmed at the inflammation of anti-semitism; Picquart and Leblois; Scheurer-Kestner and Ranc. The accusers, with the single exception of Henry, were acting in good faith. That they were precipitate is true, but in 1894 they had good reason, at the moment when the defence plans were being completely redrawn and the new 75-millimetre quick-firing field-gun, the best in Europe, was on the point of being produced. That the leading staff officers persisted in error is excusable, in that Picquart could offer no serious evidence against Esterhazy other than the handwriting, which was contro-verted by the experts, while on paper Esterhazy had an excellent record. That they were deceived may argue foolishness but not bad faith. There is no evidence of a "plot," even as regards their depositions at the Zola trial and the subsequent pro-ceedings. The transcripts of the evidence demonstrate fully that no serious consulta-tion had taken place between the generals. As for the famous conspiracy against the Republic, which Dreyfusard literature wearisomely repeats, no officer's name has ever been mentioned except Pellieux's, and that by Déroulède after the General's death.

Anti-semitism appears to have played no part in the case until Drumont and the Assumptionists took advantage of the fact that Dreyfus was a Jew. And, as Mazel remarks, anti-semitism throughout was no more than an accessory. Anti-semitic preju-dice existed both before and after the case — there are anti-semites today in all Western countries — but the fury died away, and Socialist critics as much as clerical lamented that the Jews were in fact the profiteers from the misfortunes of their co-religionist. Except for Reinach, Bernard Lazare and a few young intellectuals as yet of small importance — Marcel Proust, the Halévy brothers, Léon Blum, the Na-tansons, the circles of Mme Caillavet and Mme Strauss (Bizet's widow) — the Jews were at best neutral, and on the whole

hostile to the cause of revision. Léon Blum speaks of the egotistic and timorous pru-dence of Jewish society. "The rich Jews, the middle bourgeoisie, the Jewish public servants, were afraid of the fight . . . they thought only of going to ground and hid-ing."

In fact, a cool examination of the case shows that in its origins it arose partly from genuine error or deception, partly from mistaken loyalty. I have myself no doubt that Sandherr was convinced of Dreyfus's guilt. Had he had doubts he would never have rested until he discovered the real traitor; he would not have recommended that the papers should not be re-examined. Henry may have believed Dreyfus guilty, but he also knew that his deposition to the first court-martial was false. That he feared the appearance of new evidence seems clear from the fact that, six months before Pic-quart came on Esterhazy's name, he wrote the "Blenheim" letter: none other than he had an interest in sending it. His subse-quent forgeries and manipulations were pursued in the spirit of loyalty to the Army and the Statistical Section and with the intention of stiffening his superiors. That such conduct was not unique is shown by André, who in his memoirs quotes letters from his personal secretariat which indicate that they were pushing him forward by acting behind his back. As for Henry, the actions of a single cunning, stupid man, with his own conception of loyalty, pre-cipitated a political crisis of great magni-tude in which he involved his chiefs and in the end brought about the dissolution of the department he was striving to fortify.

The second phase of the Affair turns on the Zola trial. This led to the entry of the intellectuals, particularly the teachers and students of the École Normale Supérieure. I have no doubt in my own mind, although the only evidence is that of his biographer, Charles Andler, that the real fomenter of the tumult was Lucien Herr, the School's librarian, the mentor and inspirer of Jaurès. The reactions of this group are not invari-ably as would be expected. Barrès, as

Benda acutely saw, by turning anti-revisionist denied both his past and his nature. He had not been a devotee of order as preferable to justice, but "the cultivator of anti-social individualism." In consequence "he never felt completely happy, as if he were poisoned by the bitterness of a secret betrayal, treachery to himself." In contrast to Barrès, Clemenceau, temperamentally authoritarian, who within ten years of his adoption of Dreyfus's cause was showing himself the ruthless adept of *raison d'état*, fought with indomitable spirit on the side which his ruling passion must have told him was wrong because it was against authority.

The third phase is that of the professional politicians. Throughout they behaved with the familiar opportunism of politicians: but opportunism is a natural part of politics. In the early period they no more than the general public could penetrate the truth. Practically the whole Chamber thankfully accepted Cavaignac's assurances. But after Henry's suicide they displayed all the *canaillerie* of opportunism, and their later assumption of virtue is as revolting as their unscrupulous attacks on the Church and the Army and the creation of the fantasy of a clerico-military plot. How little they were concerned with the justice they talked of is to be seen in their behaviour after the pardon of 1899, when for more than three years the majority blocked every move to reopen the case.

The political consequences of the Affair horrified many of the early revisionists. Reinach, while remaining a faithful fighter for Dreyfus, shows in his sixth volume, written after the final rehabilitation, his distress at Dreyfusardism and its aftermath. Like many others, he had hoped to avoid the consequences of his actions. It was not to be, and no one has more clearly summed up the Dreyfusist blindness than Julien Benda. "Those who persist in dissociating the judicial Dreyfus case from the political do not wish to see that if they in all sincerity made the dissociation, the mob did not, could not make it, with the result that their judicial action, whether they desired it or not, became inevitably a political action. The single coherent attitude for the non-revolutionary Dreyfusist was to say *either:* 'I put justice before all, and *with death in my soul* accept the political consequences of my act of justice'; *or* 'I put order above everything, and *with death in my soul* renounce an act of justice which will inevitably bring in its train such and such social consequences.' As for claiming to carry out the act which they believed just, while avoiding the social troubles, it was, if done in good faith, a demonstration, as Maurras clearly saw, of blindness very near to weakness of mind."

In his reminiscences, Lord Morley remarked that it was difficult to see how Acton reconciled the view that history is a matter of broad general principles with his other view that the real prize of the historian is the episode on the back-stairs. The Affair illustrates the reconciliation. The secret actions of a minor executive official began a movement which ended in a great transformation of the political scene. Yet, even so, chance played an enormous part, intervening on more than one occasion with shattering effect. But for chance, Dreyfus would have died on The Devil's Island, a dishonoured man. As the old police agent in Nizan's *La Conspiration* says: "Little chances and little men manufacture great events. The masses and the professors never see the true relationship because the causes have no visible proportion to the consequences, and all the tracks are blurred. Everyone is blind to the turns and twists of chance and the secret of little men."

Again, the Affair illustrates the influence of propaganda on history. Nine-tenths of the literature of the case is Dreyfusard; the Dreyfusard view, with its crude blacks and whites, has passed into history. The anti-Dreyfusard versions, such as they are, are no less propagandist, but since their side was defeated, the writers have been ineffective. Both versions are distorted. It is only by examining the case in detail that a picture emerges, not of virtue at grips with villainy, but of fallible human beings pulled this way and that by their beliefs, their loyalties, their prejudices, their ambitions and their ignorance. *"Rien ne vit que par le détail."*

IV. CONTEXT AND CONSEQUENCES

The Larger Issues Joined

FRANÇOIS GOGUEL

THE Dreyfus Affair occupies a very eminent place in the history of the Third Republic. This results partly from its complications, but above all because it provided the occasion for two systems of moral values to confront each other, and because it was in turn systematically exploited by the parties of Established Order and Movement. It has long been impossible to speak of "the Affair" without reviving the passions it once aroused. . . .

It was necessary to recall the "detective story" side of the Dreyfus Affair, because its complexity had many great repercussions. It is, however, secondary with respect to its psychological and moral aspects. The Affair shook French consciences to their depths, in opposing two conceptions of the world, or at least of society, two value systems which appeared completely irreconcilable. It is because of two great writers, Maurice Barrès on one side, Charles Péguy on the other, that we can today try to understand them.

In the eyes of those opposed to revision there was no higher value than the national interest. The term "nationalist," which then made its appearance in political and literary vocabularies, is indicative here. With the founding of the *Action Française,* royalists, too, soon ranged themselves under the banner of nationalism. The defenders of Dreyfus were essentially reproached with weakening France by shaking the confidence of the people in the Army chiefs, by sapping the authority of the courts-martial, even indirectly and violently disparaging traditionally respected military values. Many thought that such an undertaking could only have been conceived by foreigners and by Jews, French perhaps in the eyes of the law, but foreigners by race, and hence the legend of the Syndicate.

Secondary themes were grouped around this fundamental one of a national interest defined in the narrowest sense. At the time of the Affair the authority of the "rendered judgment" was much discussed. It was less a question of a juridical axiom than of a general principle of social organization. What the anti-revisionists wished to retain above all else was the prestige, the order of the authorities, that is, of all those invested by law or custom with a special power of decision and consequently, with a particular responsibility; to submit them to the influence of public opinion, whether exercised by the masses, by intellectuals, or by ordinary journalists would lead, it was thought, to anarchy. In this respect, the Dreyfus Affair was only, in brief, a new episode in the struggle which, from the end of the old regime and throughout the nineteenth century, had opposed the supporters of absolute power and the partisans of limiting the arbitrary power of the mighty. The authority to be preserved was no longer that of the king or church, nor even

From François Goguel, *La Politique des Partis sous la IIIe République* (Paris, 1946), pp. 100–103, 104, 105–106, 108–109. Reprinted by permission of the Éditions du Seuil. Translated by the editor.

that of the nobility, but rather that of the Army chiefs. In a country where all dynastic loyalty had little by little disappeared, where secular powers had obtained a strong position, where the "new classes" possessed all avenues to power, but where patriotism remained active and where sympathy for the Army was general, one could hope that the military terrain would furnish the best point of departure for the general restoration of the prestige of social authority. Royalists and clericals would not be deceived; all that remained of the former, all within or near the Church who wished it to play a political role, came out against revision, along with nationalist and military circles.

The absolute confidence in all those invested with power, simply because the maintenance of the social order demanded that their prestige always remain intact, was related to a decided aversion for the methods of control which others would have wished to impose. It is not by chance that Maurice Barrès, for whom intelligence was only a "poor little thing on the surface of ourselves," became the most eminent of the nationalist writers. The Dreyfus Affair provoked the crystallization of the anti-intellectual reaction called forth by the scientific excesses of the nineteenth century. It was in the name of instinct, of obscure and profound forces of being, it was in mocking the pretensions of an exaggerated rationalism that one refused to listen to the arguments which proved the innocence of Dreyfus. That was true less perhaps because of the objective elements of the Affair — it is not certain that all the anti-revisionists believed in Dreyfus' guilt — than for reasons of a more general order; it would have appeared dangerous to allow the intellectuals, writers, professors, people living in an abstract universe without rapport with the real world, to have a controlling voice in affairs. It was the traditional suspicion of the patrician, the businessman, the "realist," for the intellectual who aligns himself too easily with reasoning or with ideas, but whom one suspects of being, at

bottom, a sophist. Many professors, notably Chartists and historians, would wish to study a contemporary affair and apply to it the critical methods elaborated by erudition, used to resolve wholly abstract problems; such pretension seemed to a good many people both presumptuous and scandalous.

But it was above all against the revisionist conception of the individual, of justice, and of liberty that their opponents raised themselves. Was it legitimate to disturb profoundly social order and public peace and threaten national cohesion to prevent an innocent man from being submitted to an unjust punishment? Such was the moral problem raised by the Dreyfus Affair. It is told how, at the time of the subscription opened by *La Libre Parole* to offer a sword of honor to Colonel Henry's widow, the writer Paul Léautaud sent a gift accompanied by the indorsement, "For order, against justice and truth." This was to pose the problem in terms too brutal to be admitted at the time, but nevertheless exact. The anti-revisionist camp grouped all who leaned towards settling the Affair in favor of order, that is, of justice rendered to the rights of the collectivity in preference to those of an isolated individual.

To these higher motives for the anti-revisionist attitude, others must be added; aversion for Israelites, suspicion of civilians by the military, leaning towards peremptory affirmations against pretensions of the critical spirit, and finally, the wish to exploit patriotic sentiment and indignation against the "traitor" for the sake of a plebiscitary *coup d'état* (this was the case of Déroulède), or of a monarchical restoration (at the time of Félix Faure's funeral, the Duke of Orléans was at the French frontier).

Degree by degree, in the huge throng of those opposing revision, the anti-intellectualism of a man as intelligent as Barrès became the instinctive hatred of the imbecile for those whose faculties are superior to his; doctrinal anti-semitism was transformed into irrational and jealous aversion for Israelites who had succeeded; the affirmation of the primacy of the national interest was transformed into the oversimplified and brutal negation of the most elementary right of the citizen to the equity and impartiality of his judges.

Similar differences are found between the motives of some partisans of revision and those in the majority. . . . Not all the revisionists displayed the sentiments of a Péguy and his sense of national honor. . . . The first ones, Picquart, Zola, continued to follow their own professions as best they were able. But the great majority could not resist the singular temptation to exert enormous influence, intense, concentrated, condensed, like an oil-spot on water, having considerable effect in small quantity and for a small initial effort. . . .

There were in fact among them, from the outset, men less concerned with the fate of an innocent man, victim of a judicial error, and with the "eternal health of France," than with wishing to speed-up the evolution which for a century was submitting most public institutions to popular control; it was useful, in their eyes, to ruin the prestige of the council of war and to introduce a "democratic" spirit into the Army, to make it hostile to secret procedures, to traditional hierarchies, and even to simple discipline. Anti-militarism was perhaps born, as Bainville thought, in the reform by which intellectuals were drafted into military service, and suffered from it more than peasants and workers; at the outset it was certainly one of the most powerful and widespread motives of the revisionists. Of all the public institutions, since the expurgation of the magistracy, the Army remained under the Republic what it had been during the dynastic regimes; the error committed by the court-martial of 1894 presented an opportunity to transform its spirit. . . .

The Affair was thus entered into in two ways at the same time; from both the moral, and because it could be exploited, the political point of view. Can one dismiss the two parties equally, however, and consider their responsibilities the same in light of the passionate struggles caused by the Dreyfus Affair and in the consequences that they had for France?

I do not think so. In spite of the legend of the syndicate, priority in the wish to exploit the Affair politically certainly devolves on the anti-revisionists. Since 1894 the anti-semitic campaigns of *La Libre Parole* had contributed to the judicial launching of the accusation against Dreyfus, and perhaps also to the irregularities which permeated his condemnation. In the course of the following years, deputies of Boulangist origin knew at once the steps taken by the Dreyfus family to obtain the revision of his trial and the refusal of the General Staff; the first interpellation on the Affair was made in 1896 by an anti-revisionist. These facts constituted elements of particular responsibility for adversaries of revision. The prestige of the Army chiefs could only have been enhanced if they had accepted gracefully the error committed in 1894. One would above all have had to subtract from political passions a question which could have remained strictly legal.

In addressing themselves to the War Office, on the contrary, Mathieu Dreyfus and Bernard Lazare proved that in asking them to revise the trial, they did not conceive of exploiting the Affair politically. Afterwards they canvassed the parliamentarians; due to practices consecrated by the Republic it was natural to count on the actions of deputies and senators to obtain a decision, which, left to itself, the administration had first refused. When Scheurer-Kestner went to see Méline and General Billot, it was not yet partisan exploitation of a judicial problem. It was after his letter to *Le Temps*, following the interpellation of 1897 in the Chamber and Senate, that the development of anti-militarist themes by journalists on the left campaigning for revision inaugurated the period of political exploitation of the Dreyfus Affair. The formation of the Brisson-Cavaignac Cabinet showed, however, that in June, 1898, the principal chiefs of the left had not yet decided to take part.

Beginning in August, 1898, it seems to me that the responsibility should be equally divided. The mass entry of socialists and radicals into the revisionist camp, the rallying of more and more numerous parliamentarians, almost as far as the Progressists, all indicate that the Party of Movement had then resolved to use the Dreyfus Affair for political ends. The activities of the Duke of Orléans, who reached the French frontier the day of Félix Faure's funeral, the tentative *coup d'état* of Déroulède, show that, on their part, royalists and plebiscitarians also wanted to use it as a means of overthrowing the parliamentary republic.

But to the degree that the success of the revisionists was affirmed, it is on their side that exploitation of the Affair for political purposes tended increasingly to remove it from the originally disinterested motives.

Priority in the wish to exploit it therefore falls to the anti-revisionists. But effective and successful exploitation is finally the accomplishment of their adversaries. By an apparent paradox, the Dreyfusard *mystique* is little by little degraded into a Dreyfusard *politique*, but the nationalist *politique* is progressively elevated until it became a national *mystique*. Hence the difficulty experienced today in judging the protagonists of the drama; to condemn totally the attitude of Barrès appears almost as difficult, even if one believes Dreyfus innocent, as to disapprove of the action of Péguy. . . .

The extraordinary violence of the passions unleashed by the Dreyfus Affair did not allow the rupture between republicans of the left and of the right to be short-lived. In addition to interests, principles

had been involved; moreover, the Affair, once ended, left with the victors an inexplicable animosity, with the vanquished, wounds that were long to heal. One stone more was added to the wall raised between the parties of France by Boulangism, the sixteenth of May, the Commune, the second of December, and the June days.

Waldeck's majority was constituted for a precise object, the safety of the regime and the end of agitation; but this being attained, it had to seek means of survival. That called for a program to reconcile the heterogeneous elements which formed it. In spite of the worthy effort made by Millerand at the Ministry of Commerce, the terrain of understanding was not that of social policy. The difference was too great between collectivists of the socialist party and the impenitent individualists of the Democratic Alliance. As for those who perhaps could have proposed new measures of social organization which would not be new factors in the class struggle, the Catholics (still few in number) who embraced the spirit of the Encyclical *Rerum Novarum,* they were automatically relegated to the opposition by virtue of the role played by too many elements of the Church in the Dreyfus Affair.

Thus, it was in anti-clerical action, and soon anti-Catholic, that the Waldeck-Rousseau majority naturally sought the means to perpetuate itself; this program alone would not be deeply resented by any of its groupings.

Anti-republican agitation, militarist and clerical manoeuvering at the time of the Dreyfus Affair had not only therefore consolidated — some say actually founded — the Republic and divided the Army; it revived the most violent anti-religious sectarianism.

The Coming of a "New Deal" to French Politics

RUDOLPH A. WINNACKER

Rudolph Winnacker, after a career in college teaching, is presently chief historian in the Office of the Secretary of Defense. He has written occasional but important articles on recent French history, one of which was an early bibliography of historical accounts of the Third Republic. In the following selection he shows how political developments in France were affected by the Dreyfus Affair.

THE Dreyfus Affair is usually considered a turning point in the history of the Third French Republic. In the opinion of many the success of the Dreyfusards marks the final victory of the ideals of the French Revolution over those of the *Ancien Régime*. Such an important result seems to indicate that a political revolution took place in France during the years 1898–99. The facts, however, do not bear out this conjecture. Neither an electoral victory nor a fundamental realignment of parties made the success of the Dreyfusards possible. The Dreyfus Affair merely speeded up a movement in French politics which had been gathering force since the beginning of the last decade of the nineteenth century.

The election of 1893 marked the first great republican victory since the establishment of the Republic. Only seventy-eight Monarchists and Boulangists were elected as opposed to five hundred and three supporters of the republican form of government. This large majority, however, was not homogeneous. After a period of trial and error which furnished five ministries between 1893 and 1895, it split into two parts: one in favor of a conservative republic, the other supporting a radical policy. The latter was by far the weaker. It

was able to control the government for only six months, from November, 1895, to April, 1896, when it gave way to an alliance of the conservative forces under Méline, who kept his majority together until after the elections of 1898. The composition and the policies of these two political combinations must be explained, for they represent the divisions which are usually considered the result of the Dreyfus Affair.

The main strength of the conservative forces came from the republican group, known as Progressist. The deputies of this group were satisfied with the Republic as Thiers had established it, a monarchy without a king, an individualistic, *antiétatiste* régime of the upper classes, opposed to social legislation. *Ni révolution, ni réaction* was their slogan. To safeguard the conservative Republic they worked for the conversion of Monarchists and Catholics to republicanism by a policy of *apaisement*. They hoped that with the help of these *ralliés* a conservative majority could be established which would liberate them from the annoying alliance with the Radicals. Though some sixty members of the group had their doubts about the sincerity of the new converts, most of them followed Méline from 1896 to 1898, when this prime

Reprinted from "The Influence of the Dreyfus Affair on the Political Development of France," pp. 465–68, 472–78, in *Papers of the Michigan Academy of Science, Arts, and Letters*, XXX (Ann Arbor, 1936), by Rudolph A. Winnacker by permission of The University of Michigan Press. Copyright, 1936, by the University of Michigan.

minister put into effect the conservative policy called the *esprit nouveau*.

The opposing faction was known as the Union of the Lefts, composed of the Radical, the Radical-Socialist, and the Socialist groups. The Radicals traced their political pedigree back to Gambetta's program of Belleville, proposed in 1869, but as realists they saw the impossibility of gathering a majority in the near future to realize such reforms as the separation of State and churches, an income tax, the election of judges and other civil servants. Consequently they were eager to cooperate with the Progressists whenever possible in dividing the spoils of office. The Radical-Socialists, on the other hand, acted as if they believed in the Belleville program. They refused to compromise with the Progressists and considered themselves the spiritual heirs of the Jacobins of 1792, claiming to be the prophets of the democratic, laïcal, and fraternal republic of the future. The third group in this union consisted of various factions sailing under the flag of socialism. Temporarily discouraged by the fate of the Commune of 1871, these champions of the proletariat had gathered by 1890 a new feeling of hope and courage, based on the gospel of Marx and the memories of Babeuf, Louis Blanc, and Blanqui.

The election of 1898 was to test the strength of these two alliances. Since the Dreyfus Affair was still in its early stages and played only a minor part, the great issue was between conservatism and radicalism. The result, however, was far from decisive. Neither the Progressists nor the Union of the Lefts could muster a majority in the Chamber of Deputies. The importance of the election, therefore, does not appear in the actual election returns. It is to be sought in the attitude of the two groups at the extreme right and left of parliament. In the first place, the hostility of some Monarchists toward their recent allies, the Progressists, had resulted in the defeat of two of Méline's ministers and nearly twenty of his followers. Secondly, the Socialists, by tacitly accepting Millerand's famous minimum program of St. Mandé, had lost the stigma of revolutionism and taken their place in the parliamentary republic as a party of reform. Thus the foundations had been laid for a future alliance between the deputies of the left wing of the Progressist group and the Union of the Lefts. The former, who had been undecided whether the Monarchists or the Socialists presented the greater peril to the Republic, now had grave doubts regarding Méline's *esprit nouveau* policy and looked upon the Socialists as less dangerous to the bourgeoisie than before.

This result of the election became evident as soon as Méline faced the new Chamber. On June 14, 1898, the deputies approved the general policy followed by Méline during the past two years by a majority of twenty-three, but at the same time passed a resolution calling for a cabinet "supported exclusively by republicans." Since the majority on the first vote had included over eighty Monarchists and Ralliés, Méline was forced to resign. All attempts to create a cabinet based on the cooperation of Radicals and Progressists failed. The animosities created during the electoral campaign were too deep to be forgotten immediately. Something approaching the two-party system seemed to be in formation in France, as the Progressist Méline was succeeded by a cabinet of the Union of the Lefts, headed by Brisson. This change in the government of France was made possible only by the vacillations of nearly forty deputies of the left wing of the Progressist group who first had supported Méline, but who later cast their lot with the groups of the left.

It appears from these events that even before the Dreyfus Affair threw France into turmoil the French parliament was divided into two hostile camps. Therefore, the *bloc* of the Lefts ought not to be considered a product of this crisis, since a similar political alliance was in existence during the years from 1895 to 1898. Likewise the Progressist group, which practically disintegrated during the critical days of 1899, had in fact started its decline immediately after the elections of the previous year. In other words, the final political result of the Dreyfus Affair was not the break-up of the old political alignments, but the reënforcement of existing divisions. . . .

The fall of Dupuy [June, 1899] opened the most important ministerial crisis in the twenty odd years of the existence of the Third Republic. The events of the last few months seemed to indicate that the solution of the crisis lay in a government of the left, but the Dreyfus Affair had raised the passions of the opposing factions to such a pitch that a nonpartisan government seemed more likely to survive the crisis. The retrial of Dreyfus was bound to increase the excitement. Not only was a strong leader needed to steer France through this period of storm and stress, but the conditions also demanded an unusual amount of political sagacity among the deputies of the Chamber. Conservatives and radicals would have to forget their differences temporarily. The time for the usual dickering of offices and spoils had passed. The groups which showed the greatest wisdom and unity at this time would inevitably be considered the saviors of France.

As the man best fitted to overcome the present and future troubles, the president of the Republic chose the Progressist senator Waldeck-Rousseau. The latter, however, insisted that the thirty-eight-year-old Raymond Poincaré should make the first attempt at solving the crisis. The young Progressist negotiated for six days, but his desire to keep his own party in power led to his failure. The Radicals were promised only two ministries. Even the present complications could not turn the deputies of the left into political ascetics. Waldeck-Rousseau was the next to try his hand, but this time the senator's own party prevented a solution of the crisis. The Progressists refused to agree with Waldeck-Rousseau in considering the Republic sufficiently endangered to justify the inclusion of the

Socialist Millerand in the cabinet. By constantly increasing their demands for guarantees against the Socialists they finally turned a statesmanlike conception into a failure. Two more days were wasted in trying to find a Radical to take the leadership, but to no avail. The Radicals, usually only too anxious to replace the Progressists in the government, were loath to assume responsibility at the present critical hour. It was after these none too savory developments that Waldeck-Rousseau performed his "leap in the dark."

On June 22, 1899, he formed a cabinet without consulting his own party, the Progressists. Impressed by the seriousness of the crisis and sick of the system of mutual guarantees and petty bickerings, he gathered his collaborators from the four corners of the political horizon. Not only did the cabinet include the Socialist Millerand to enrage the Progressists, but its minister of war was no other than the Marquis de Galliffet, the butcher of the Commune, hated by the Socialists more than any other general in the French army. Moreover, the Radicals, who were expected to furnish more than half of the majority, had to be satisfied with only two out of eleven ministerial positions. The cabinet seemed to have been formed purposely to test the self-denial of the republicans.

Under these critical circumstances the groups of the left showed the greatest cohesion. The Radicals and Radical-Socialists decided to vote for Waldeck-Rousseau in spite of the unfavorable division of spoils, for the failure of their so-called leaders to attempt a solution of the crisis had left them no other choice. Among the Socialists, however, the new cabinet created the deepest divisions. Jaurès and his twenty-five followers were willing to support Waldeck-Rousseau for the sake of the Republic and in the hope of future social legislation. To Guesde and the remaining Socialists, on the other hand, Millerand's appointment represented merely another attempt of the capitalists to disarm the proletariat, and therefore the new government did not deserve, even in this crisis, the approval of the true disciples of Marx.

Thus Waldeck-Rousseau could count on nearly two hundred votes from the Union of the Lefts; at least eighty more were needed to assure the defense of the Republic, and these had to come from Waldeck-Rousseau's own group, the Progressists. The united support of this group would have freed the prime minister from a too great dependence on the Radicals, but such a far-sighted policy the Progressists were unable to adopt. Some were Dreyfusards, others anti-Dreyfusards. Some considered the Socialists the greatest danger to France, others the Monarchists and the Nationalists. Consequently when Waldeck-Rousseau asked the Chamber of Deputies for its confidence on June 26, 1899, only eighty-six Progressists voted for him, while one hundred and two opposed him and thirty-one abstained from voting. Still this split among the Progressists was large enough to save the new cabinet from defeat. Its vague program of "Republican Defense," cooperation, and pacification was approved by the narrow majority of twenty-four votes.

With this slight margin of safety Waldeck-Rousseau entered upon his task of reëstablishing order in France. By arresting twenty-three of the most prominent Nationalists he deprived the antirepublican forces of their leaders. The Dreyfus Affair was temporarily liquidated in a manner which satisfied neither the Nationalists nor the Dreyfusards and consequently was probably the best solution for the internal peace of France. Galliffet restored the discipline in the army. By November, 1899, the crisis had been met successfully. But did the re-establishment of temporary order end the task of Waldeck-Rousseau? Was not the government of Republican Defense duty-bound to prevent any possible recurrence of the late troubles? Waldeck-Rousseau felt that the answer to the latter question could be only in the affirmative.

The periodic attacks against the Republic in 1877, 1889, and 1899 had involved the same political and social factions: the Church, the army, and the civil service. It seemed obvious that these perennial enemies of the established institutions had to be rendered harmless or trouble was bound to occur again. The republicanization of the army, a change in the procedure of military courts, a new procedure in the recruitment of civil servants, all these measures seemed necessary to assure the safety of the Republic. Above all, however, it was the Church which claimed the government's attention. For the third time it had supported the antirepublican forces almost unanimously. The destruction of the educational and political power of the clergy seemed to be a prerequisite for the internal peace of France. It was a program inspired by these ideas that Waldeck-Rousseau decided to adopt. This decision was to influence the political life of France for the next ten years.

To the political parties in the Chamber the prime minister's new program presented new and serious difficulties. To vote for a government of Republican Defense in a serious crisis was a simple matter compared to the question whether or not to support a government of Republican Attack over a number of years. The Radicals and Radical-Socialists were still chagrined by their underrepresentation in the cabinet, but they realized that they did not possess the necessary majority to form their own government. Moreover, the cabinet's new program was enough like their own platform to deserve their full support, and they could desire no better advertisement than the endorsement of the formerly conservative Waldeck-Rousseau. In the Socialist camp the schism created in June, 1899, continued, but even the "pure" Socialists were willing to support the social reforms of the cabinet, though reserving their freedom of action on any issue conflicting with Socialist principles. Thus the government could count on the support of the entire Union of the Lefts, about two hundred and twenty votes, for the realization of its program.

Among the political groups the Progressists were faced with the greatest dilemma. Though the majority of the ministers were affiliated with this group, the program of the cabinet was contrary to the policy followed by the Progressists for two years under Méline. After having fought and denounced the Socialists, they were now asked to accept them as their allies. They had hoped and worked for the conversion of the Monarchists and the Catholic clergy to republicanism, and now the latter were to be persecuted. Méline and one hundred and twenty of his followers were unable to make this change. To them the Dreyfus Affair had merely proved the weakness of the antirepublicans, who, if only let alone, would die a natural death. More and more Progressists, however, agreed with Waldeck-Rousseau that the recent events necessitated a new policy. Ever since the elections of 1898 deputies had been leaving the Progressist group; some were impressed by their electoral experience, others by the revelations of the Dreyfus case, which had shown the extreme conservatives as inveterate enemies of the Republic. All of them, however, realized that their chances of re-election would be enhanced by obtaining the support of Radicals. These Progressist dissenters, numbering over eighty in November, 1899, were to be the main support of Waldeck-Rousseau.

Consequently, when the Chamber of Deputies approved Waldeck-Rousseau's program on November 14, 1899, the political consequnces of the Dreyfus Affair became clear. The stage was set for a "New Deal" in French politics through the emergence of the Union of the Lefts as the controlling factor within the French parliament. In existence ever since the first years of the decade, this alliance of Radicals, Radical-Socialists, and Socialists had grown from a minority into a majority party through the adhesion of the left-wing Progressists. This new combination was to be called the *bloc* of the Lefts, and its leaders were to be in power for the next ten years.

The Need to Save the Army

JACQUES CHASTENET

The most recent and perhaps most ambitious history of the Third French Republic is that of Jacques Chastenet. At first a journalist, who served as editor of one of France's most important newspapers, Le Temps, from 1931 to 1942, he has written English as well as French history, and is a member of the Académie Française. The following excerpt presents a unique interpretation of the spate of anti-clerical legislation following the Dreyfus Affair.

THE situation was serious; in order to control it, a strong government was obviously necessary. Loubet asked Poincaré to constitute one. Poincaré, leader of the Dreyfusard Moderates, enjoyed considerable prestige, but had a rather narrow outlook. He thought first in terms of the advantages to be derived by his political associates. Perhaps, aware of the difficulties of the situation, he was unable to display much conviction. In any case he failed, and the President of the Republic called on Waldeck-Rousseau.

Senator Waldeck-Rousseau was then fifty-three years old. He was a "great bourgeois," a renowned lawyer, an amateur artist, and an experienced parliamentarian. His early career had been especially facilitated by the fact that he was the son of a leading member of the early opposition to Napoleon III. He served as Minister of the Interior in the Gambetta Cabinet, and holding the same portfolio in the second Ferry Cabinet, helped enact the bill legalizing trade unions. With an elegant appearance, a somber face, motionless features, sparing in gestures and cold as ice, his speeches fell on his audiences like a cover from above. When descending from the tribunal after a successful oration, he would put his hands into his pockets to avoid having to shake those of his friends.

As caustic as Poincaré, his junior, he was more penetrating, and Poincaré, who often met him as an adversary in a courtroom, wholly admired, while fearing him. "The first time that I argued against him," he said, "I had the feeling of a poodle barking at a statue."

Politically, Waldeck-Rousseau called himself "a moderate republican but not moderately republican." If his sense of proportion kept him from the reactionary right, his tastes separated him no less from the far left. Above all, he was a man of order, a man of government, a jurist imbued with a sense of the state.

Asked to form a government, he at once judged as the most pressing danger he would have to face, that which threatened the Army. The danger was twofold: within, discipline was threatened by whims of insubordination demonstrated by certain great chiefs; externally, it was the military institution itself, embroiled by the passion to which the obstinacy of the General Staff had afforded the pretext.

To ward off this double threat, Waldeck-Rousseau deemed it advisable first to place at the head of the Ministry of War a man enjoying as much prestige as possible in order to be obeyed without protest, then to direct towards other objectives the passions aimed at the Army.

From Jacques Chastenet, "Histoire de la Troisième République" (*La République triomphante*), Vol. III, Librairie Hachette (Paris, 1955), pp. 165–68, 176–80, 210. Translated by the editor.

Galliffet, the former "dashing cavalry officer" at imperial balls — characterized by feline flippancy, impertinence, skin stretched on the edge of bone, brick-red complexion, cat-like mustache, havoc in alcoves, mad bravery on battlefields — was known to the public at large for the merciless severity with which he had participated in the repression of the Commune. He was esteemed by specialists for the reforms he made in cavalry regulations. Although an aristocrat to his fingertips, but devoid of prejudice, he had previously made the acquaintance of Gambetta, through the intermediary of the Prince of Wales, and fell under the charm of the great tribune. His career had been brilliant, but insufficient to satisfy all his ambitions. Boulanger and his demogogic chauvinism had disgusted him; the manoeuvers of the General Staff during the Dreyfus Affair seemed absurd to him.

In fact, from his lofty and ennobled vantage point, he viewed the anti-Dreyfusard generals with no less detachment than freemason politicians. His scorn was widespread, as evidenced by his remark about the Russian grand-dukes: "They are stupid, those people, and moreover, their family is inferior to mine." The aloofness of Waldeck-Rousseau pleased him, and when the latter asked his cooperation, the old, but ever brilliant cavalier without hesitation agreed to serve.

The granting of a portfolio to the "fusilier" of 1871 risked being viewed by the extreme left as a provocation. By way of an antidote, Waldeck thought of Millerand, the solid and gruff lawyer-journalist, the theoretician of parliamentary socialism, and the author of the Saint-Mandé speech which had made the propertied bourgeoisie tremble in threatening them with legal expropriation. Millerand had begun to be weary of useless polemics; he aspired to action and promised his cooperation. It was then that the old communard, Vaillant, keeper of the Blanquist tradition, wrote to him:

"It is said that you will enter a minis-

terial combination with Galliffet . . . That appears to me so odious, so ignoble, that I cannot believe it and I hope at the earliest to be reassured."

On the other hand, Viviani and Briand, two newly elected socialists, already influential and very ambitious, sensed how important it was to their careers for men of their party to cease being political pariahs; their approval of Millerand led to that of a number of their colleagues.

But for three days, as a result of conditions that the Moderates persisted in imposing, everything seemed destined to fall apart. Loubet had Léon Bourgeois come from The Hague where he was representing France at the disarmament conference, but the unctuous octogenarian of radicalism found it less dangerous to secure the peace of the world than that of France, and he departed in haste for the Low Countries. The crisis was perpetuated, threatening to end in disaster, but at last, on June 22, having received a new mandate from the Élysée, Waldeck-Rousseau presented a government.

He took for himself, with the presidency of the council, the portfolio of Interior and Cults. Galliffet received that of War; Millerand, Commerce and Industry; and Delcassé was retained at Foreign Affairs. Finance was confided to the young and prancing Joseph Caillaux; Education fell to Georges Leygues, the amiable and cultivated displayer of beautiful mustaches; Agriculture went to Jean Dupuy, important for his ownership of *Le Petit Parisien,* the most widespread French newspaper. There were only eleven ministers in all, and no under-secretaries of state.

If, in this Cabinet, Moderates of a Dreyfusian tinge were in the majority, its most conspicuous members were the Ministers of War and of Commerce. When on June 26, the Cabinet appeared before the Chamber, it was greeted with an uproar. Socialists inveighed against Galliffet and howled, "Long live the Commune! Down with the assassin!" Progressists booed Millerand; Progressive Radicals pouted at

Waldeck-Rousseau; the impartial distributed their abuse equally.

In its declaration the Government solicited the "cooperation of all republicans to put an end to directed agitation, obviously disguised, against the regime consecrated to universal suffrage," and claimed "the most extensive mandate."

The words were coolly received. It was doubtful that a vote of confidence would be obtained. But at the last moment the great Lyon banker Aynard, Catholic and liberal, persuaded about twenty Progressists to join the republicans of the left and vote for Waldeck-Rousseau. Brisson acted similarly with the free-masons; Briand and Viviani, with the Socialists. The Cabinet finally carried the vote 263 to 237.

It was a weak majority, but a significant one since it threw back into the opposition not only the *"ralliés"* but a good part of the Progressists. Although the President of the Council and most of his ministers were moderates, the majority, which knew no enemies on the left, was virtually based on radicalism; discreetly at first, then openly, it began to control French public life for fifteen years. From this point of view, the vote of June 26, 1899, marked, in the history of political affairs, a cardinal date. . . .

Although not yet cured of the fever which had just attacked it, the country — at least the legal country — refused to seek satisfaction by means of useful, but unspectacular, reforms. What was needed were dramatic flashes, appeals to principles, a bustle of general ideas, and, at the same time, personal denunciations, vengeances, defamations; in short, pure politics.

During the autumn of 1899, this need was satisfied by the spectacle afforded by the Senate, constituted as a high court, in judging the fifteen members of the different Leagues accused of weakening the security of the State. (A selection had been made, and some highly placed military officials were not indicted, despite the existence of strong opinions to the contrary.)

In the course of the forty-seven sittings neither the indignant protests of the interested parties, nor the brawls among witnesses, nor the vehement if eloquent outbursts, constituted a default. Only the *bonhomie* of the cordial Fallières, who had succeeded Loubet as President of the High Assembly, prevented the outbreak of pitched battles. Finally, it appeared that the famous conspiracies were of no great importance, and most of the accused were acquitted. Only Déroulède, president of the League of Patriots, André Buffet, chief of the political bureau of the Duke of Orléans, and Jules Guerin, president of the Anti-Semitic League, were condemned; the first two to ten years exile, the last to ten years detention.

That would hardly suffice, however, to appease the anger of the left. Now that Galliffet had undertaken the necessary measures, Waldeck-Rousseau wished above all to shelter the Army from this bitterness. In what direction then, to divert it? Towards big business? But Waldeck-Rousseau and most of the members of his majority were social conservatives. Towards the powers of high finance? But it was necessary to seek vengeance on anti-Dreyfusards, and a good part of the banking world was in the Dreyfusard camp. Towards the tariff system of 1892, so unfavorable to consumers? But the peasants, who constituted the bulk of the electorate, would certainly reject anything interfering with their protective tariff. Generally speaking, about 80% of the French people still trembled at the very mention of socialism.

Then towards what? It was then that "clericalism" naturally came to mind, the hatred of which had so long served as common denominator for the different groupings of the republican party. And one thought especially of the male religious congregations which, on the one hand, had never ceased to act politically in favor of the right, and on the other, shaped the minds of a great part of the young French bourgeoisie. There was the enemy begging to be attacked; one could rest assured that any blows aimed at it would be applauded by all republicans.

Under penalty of losing his weak parliamentary majority, Waldeck-Rousseau could not dispense with taking such action. Furthermore, his juridical temperament, imbued with the superiority of civil power, encouraged him. However, because he was in no way sectarian, he did not wish to be forced to move too far.

At the time of the elections of 1898, the small but opulent Congregation of Augustinians of the Assumption was directed by Father Bailly and, despite the counsels of prudence given by the nunciature, showed itself especially active. It was particularly concerned with tightening the alliance between the old right and the anti-Dreyfusard nationalists. Its multiple newspapers and its "justice-equality" committees waged a bitter campaign against republicans, whether progressive or moderate, if suspected of being attached to the lay school. Since that time the same newspapers, the same committees, violently declared themselves against revision of the Dreyfus trial and did not cease to vituperate pell-mell Jews, Protestants, free-masons, and Catholics favorable to revision. Herein lay the rash actions unable to be forgotten by the victors.

On Waldeck-Rousseau's orders the police perquisitioned the offices of *La Croix,* chief organ of the Assumptionists. Immediately afterwards, the Fathers were prosecuted before the Correctional Tribunal for infraction of Article 291 of the Penal Code which prohibited, without government authorization, the establishment of any association of more than twenty persons.

In January, 1900, the Congregation of the Augustinians of the Assumption was dissolved by sentence. It was the only one that was really seditious. But the parliamentary majority showed no signs of stopping; it wanted to take up the ideas of Jules Ferry and tear away, as much as possible, the youth, at least the male youth, from the influence of the Church (an influence especially marked in secondary educa-

tion; religious establishments offering competent teaching, including small seminaries, counted 91,000 students; lay establishments, only 86,000).

The Government had submitted two bills the preceding November. The first imposed on all candidates to public office the obligation to prove that they had spent their last three years of study in a state establishment. (It was a matter of preventing the Jesuits from preparing candidates for the great military schools.) The second acknowledged the principle of free association for all citizens except for members of the regular clergy; the associations formed by them — these are the congregations — would have to seek under penalty of dispersion, while still not formally being recognized, authorization granted by a decree issued by the Council of State.

The first bill, prompted by functionaries in the Ministry of Education, would, if adopted, deal a mortal blow to free establishments in secondary education. The Government had submitted it above all "for the sake of form." The moderates in its majority hesitated to give approval, and it was finally buried.

In revenge, the committee dealing with the second bill — the personal work of Waldeck-Rousseau — sought to increase it considerably by substituting for the authorization by decree, authorization by legislative approval. The President of the Council took advantage of the approaching Universal Exposition to delay the opening of public debate.

In January, 1900, the left was strengthened by the success obtained at the time of the partial renewal of the Senate. Of ninety-nine seats, it held eighty; the Congregations could no longer hope to find, as in the time of Ferry, support at the Luxembourg.

They tried to defend themselves. With the approval of the bishops, numerous monks, preaching from parochial chairs, denounced the government bills. Waldeck-Rousseau, questioned in the Chamber, stated that the non-authorized Congregations were "not indispensable to the well-being of the Church, and could be fatal to the well-being of the State." He was given a vote of confidence "to pursue energetically a policy of republican reforms and the defense of the laic State." The battle was begun. . . .

By returning some of the gaiety to Parisian life and rescuing it from a tide of provincialism, the Exposition [of 1900] almost managed to put an end to nationalist agitation. The bitterness, however, persisted, and the fear experienced by the defenders of the regime incited prolonged reprisals. Dreyfus himself, pardoned and now surrounded by some of his warmest partisans, was buried in semi-oblivion, but the passions aroused by his case remained as bellicose as ever.

Waldeck-Rousseau, cold and juridical, judged the game virtually won and was inclined to be moderate. In his desire to save the Army he had, on January 1, submitted legislation pardoning the behavior of those involved in the Affair and, consequently, protecting from any indictment the most compromised (notably General Mercier whose activities, as enumerated in the decree of the Court of Cassation ordering revision, attested to the crime of prevarication). The President of the Council was able to have the amnesty enacted, but by way of compensation he would have to make what is called "basic concessions" to a majority which, if it included in its right dissident Progressists, contained most of the Socialists in its left. This majority qualified as one of "Republican Defense," but few hesitated in referring to it as the *"bloc."* Anti-clericalism was to be the cement holding together this heterogeneous *"bloc."*

The Struggle Between the Two Frances

ROGER SOLTAU

Roger Soltau taught political science at the London School of Economics. Although not a prolific writer, his *French Political Thought in the Nineteenth Century* is another of the books indispensable to students of the period. In the section entitled, " 'L'Affaire Dreyfus:' Its Significance," he presents a strong liberal and republican interpretation.

WHO were these enemies [of Dreyfus], and how is one to account for a violence of feeling, a virulence of abuse, a letting-loose of the worst passions on a scale scarcely paralleled in any civilized country? Anti-Semitism by itself, however unscrupulously fanned, was scarcely enough to account for such a large measure of unanimity. The solution lies in the fact that the "Dreyfus case" provided a convenient rallying-ground for all those forces and parties which, for very different motives, were ready to seize any opportunity of attacking the existing order. Monarchists and Bonapartists saw in it the discrediting of the Republic; "Cæsarists," a revenge for their defeat under Boulanger; militarists, the reassertion of the "honour" of an army that had never been enthusiastic of Republicans and Radicals; aristocrats, the humiliation of a middle-class *régime;* but most of all did the clerical party believe the hour of its triumph had come at last: the treason of the Jew and his support by a band of Protestants, Freemasons, and Socialists showed to what depth a "non-Christian" nation could fall: it was all the result of anti-clericalism, and the time had come to re-Christianize France.

It will now be evident that the question of the technical guilt of Dreyfus was comparatively irrelevant. Not, of course, that the leaders of all those forces deliberately meant to invent a charge against an innocent man, but once it had been levied, and its solidity assumed (as there was every obvious reason to do from 1894 to 1896), the innocence of the accused became really *unthinkable*. Too many issues were at stake for dispassionate judgment to become possible. Dreyfus had to be guilty because the alternative was too appalling to contemplate. Many anti-Dreyfusards may well have regretted at times the enthusiasm with which they greeted his condemnation; but it was now too late to withdraw. Should the despised Jew win, a multitude of hopes were dashed to the ground, perhaps forever. The Republic would be strengthened in all its worst aspects; chances of a monarchical restoration would vanish into thin air; militarism would receive a serious setback; and the Church would be farther than ever from regaining the lost privileges. Dreyfus *must* be guilty. And every fresh assertion of his guilt made it still more impossible to look back: the burning of the boats had been absolute and no line of retreat was or ever would become possible. And even if he were innocent, some added, better he should suffer than all our cherished causes should have to be thrown on the scrap-heap.

The rank and file naturally followed the leaders. Why not believe those whom they had hitherto trusted when told that any

From Roger Soltau, *French Political Thought in the Nineteenth Century* (New Haven, 1931), pp. 346–351, 353–359. Reprinted by permission of Yale University Press.

71

alleged proof of innocence was a forgery and a lie? Why should a court-martial be mistaken? Were not a body of "officers and gentlemen" more likely to be right than a handful of Jews, Protestants, and Freemasons, however intellectually distinguished? Besides, to throw discredit on the army was "unpatriotic"; Dreyfus himself, even if innocent, would surely agree that any agitation should be eschewed that would not only weaken the prestige of the body to which he belonged, but provide the enemies of France with the most dangerous of weapons.

It was, in fact, this "hingeing" of the case on a number of the most elemental factors in national psychology which gave it this extraordinary acuteness. The "average" Frenchman of the nineties was not indeed a militarist or warmonger, but he loved the army, military parades, all the pomp and circumstance of the uniform, which was but natural in a conscription country. The army was not in his eyes a caste or class; the barracks was the great democratic equalizer, and officers were by no means exclusively of the aristocracy or even higher bourgeoisie. To criticize the army was to touch a national institution; to attack it with any violence a certain way of arousing the bitterest hostility. And the most enthusiastic Dreyfusard could scarcely pretend that the criticism of courts-martial and General Staff was kept within the limits of accuracy or good taste: the army as a whole came in for a great deal of gross and undeserved abuse which did much to jeopardize the case for revision.

Men like Gohier, in his *L'Armée contre la Nation,* denounced all officers indiscriminately as "tools of Loyola, perjurers, traitors," and did his best to create between army and nation a chasm that the circumstances did not warrant; and the blatant anti-militarism of a later period undoubtedly originated among some of the less worthy of the defenders of Dreyfus.

Anti-patriotism followed on the heels of anti-militarism. The insistence of the Conservatives on the danger to national safety

that would arise from any dragging of the case into the limelight, or from any pillorying of the army and its leaders, provoked the inevitable reaction against so distorted a conception of patriotism, and many a Dreyfusard fell into excesses of speech and writing which antagonized possible sympathizers and wounded his own friends. The fact that foreign opinion was virtually unanimously on the side of innocence was naturally exploited by believers in guilt and led to unedifying controversies from which *La Patrie* emerged badly damaged — all of which did not help Dreyfus. But undoubtedly the Church was the chief factor in the mobilization of public opinion. Of those who did not actually take sides, and these were not many, few took any steps at least to repress the activities of Catholic zealots, or their violence of language not only against Jews, Freemasons, Protestants, and other infidels, but against the few Catholics who hinted at the possibility of a mistake. Without in any sense identifying herself with the accused, the Church could have reduced the whole matter to its technical issues, and at least tried to bring into the tribunal an atmosphere somewhat less unworthy of her professed Lord. But this was not to be. "I am deeply grieved," wrote one of the few Dreyfusard clergy, "at the attitude of Catholics. Their partiality is so extreme that if any tribunal ever declares Dreyfus to be innocent they will only accuse the judges of being sold to Jews. All goes for nothing in their race-hatreds and religious antagonisms. To hear any reasonable Christian language, we are driven to Protestant or Rationalist newspapers"; and the writer concludes with prophetic insight that the Church will alone have to bear the weight of popular anger.

The Church, in fact, entered the fray with incredible partiality. "Dreyfusism became the eighth mortal sin and a new heresy." There was scarcely a pulpit that did not thunder with denunciation of the foes of the Church, traitors, and all the usual vocabulary of the anti-Semite Press. The Archbishop of Toulouse, in his Lent

Pastoral of February, 1898, spoke of "the widespread emotion at the deadly campaign which is being waged against our military leaders, at this rebellion against justice, at this attempt at clearing a traitor and accusing an innocent man." The Archbishop of Paris became the patron of the "Labarum League," an association of anti-Jewish officers, pledged to have no dealings with Jews or Freemasons. Among the subscribers to the Henry Memorial Fund were three hundred clergy, one of whom described himself as an "invalid priest who wished he could wield a sword as well as a holy-water sprinkler"; another wished for a "rug of Yiddish skin." The pillaging of Jewish houses in Algiers, the stripping of Jewish women in the street, was said by *La Croix* to be "on the orders of Christ himself," a proof being that Catholic shops were left intact. The Jesuit organ *Civilta Cattolica* in its issue of 5th February 1898 said that "the Jew was created by God to be a spy wherever treason was being plotted. . . . The real judicial error was that Jews should ever have been granted French citizenship. That law must be abrogated, not in France only but in Germany, Austria, and Italy. The Jews are masters of the Republic, which is not so much French as Hebrew. They reign over foreign as well as domestic policy; it was through Jewish money and intrigues that France abandoned to England her rights in Egypt. It was the Zionist Congress of Bâle that decided to press for the innocence of Dreyfus and formed a syndicate, financed with German money. They have bought consciences and papers all over Europe." Page after page could be filled with similar quotations, for exhuming which we are tempted to apologize to our readers; but the violence of reprisals can be understood only in relation to the violence of the onslaught. . . .

The situation was really saved by the slow building up, between 1897 and 1900, mainly outside Paris and its excited atmosphere, of a solid block of largely non-vocal public opinion which, without being en-thusiastic partisans of Dreyfus, or ardent lovers of Jews, had arrived at two deep-rooted convictions: first, that strict justice for the individual was the essential condition of any social order; secondly, that clericalism and militarism of a certain type had become real dangers to a Republican system of which they had no intention of being deprived because some people disliked Jews. This block of "Republican defence" drew its strength from three main classes: the teaching profession, the always anti-clerical *petite bourgeoisie* (small shopkeepers and clerks), and the industrial workers in the big towns.

The University had been foremost in the fray on behalf of Dreyfus. The Left Wing tendencies of the Sorbonne have been eclipsed at times, but always tend to reappear, and the Michelet-Quinet tradition has even when dormant always remained capable of sudden resurrection before the clerical menace. The attempt made by the Church in the seventies to reaffirm her control over education had aroused much of the old hostility which the Ralliément had failed to disarm. A number of Jews held University chairs and gave distinction to French scholarship, and neither anti-Semitism nor extravagant militarism were likely to find an echo in the intellectual *élite* of France. The guilt of Dreyfus was, of course, originally assumed, but it was in the University and its immediate circles that doubt first appeared: scientists used to weighing evidence, historians practised in methods of documentary criticism, soon became uneasy at the flimsiness of the proofs advanced, and at the prevailing reluctance to seek the truth, and it was not long before the University felt the full force of the anti-Dreyfusard attack. Those professors who had identified themselves with the revisionist cause were hooted and their lectures broken up; some were suspended from their functions; some virtually forced to resign. No contempt was strongly worded enough for the "intellectuals" who dared impugn the honour and sagacity of "men of action," and who meddled with matters outside their classroom. "Burn the whole place down," clamoured a manifesto that was broadcast in Paris in December, 1898; "let not a stone remain of those palaces which for the last hundred years have been distilling, drop by drop, the poison that is slowly but surely killing the social body. Let the teachers be severely punished! Let them be forced to do heavy manual work! Let them be tied up in twos in their kennels! Let them have no contact with the rest of mankind, for the moral leprosy that covers them is infectious. And when they have given up their wicked spirits, let them be buried in one common grave, from which everybody will shrink on reading the epitaph: 'They went through life doing evil.'"

The professors who had thus given the lead found an answering echo among their colleagues, often their ex-pupils, scattered all over France in secondary and elementary schools, most of them keen Republicans and distrustful of the Church. If public opinion changed so completely after 1900, this must be largely ascribed to its quiet re-education behind the scene by those teachers to whom the French, more perhaps than any other people, have looked for intellectual guidance.

The "intellectuals" provided leaders; the rank and file were found in the daily more numerous adherents of the Radical and Socialist parties. However far *La Libre Parole* and *L'Intransigeant* could lead their leaders astray, anti-clericalism had a tenacious hold in the French popular mind and memory; it was too ineradicable an element in the revolutionary tradition, and when an old Radical like Clemenceau reopened in his paper *L'Aurore* the old offensive against the excesses of the Church he was certain ultimately to rally many thousands who really detested the priest more than the Jew. And victory became assured when the young Socialist leader, Jean Jaurès, managed to persuade the mass of his followers that the Dreyfus affair was not, as was thought at first, a mere bourgeois quarrel with which the proletariat had no concern,

but a matter of life and death for Socialism no less than for Radicalism; if the Church were to triumph there was no hope for either. This Radical-Socialist combination it was that made possible the Waldeck-Rousseau Cabinet, won over recruit after recruit after 1900, and presented first Waldeck-Rousseau, then Combes with the solid majorities that enabled them to carry into the Catholic camp so terrible and ruthless a counter-offensive, and to pass the measures thanks to which the process of finally clearing the honour of the innocent, begun in 1903, was completed: in July, 1906, came the final verdict of the *Cour de Cassation* to the effect that "Dreyfus had been condemned on 9th September 1899 by the Rennes court martial on a sum-total of charges of which none could withstand scrutiny, and on the production of documents since recognized to be false, and the falsification of which was carried out in order both to create direct accusations against him and to discredit the witnesses on whom he relied"; whereupon the Court decided that "in the last analysis nothing remained of the charge brought against Dreyfus and consequently quashed the verdict of the Rennes court martial" and proclaimed that "it was by error and wrongly that condemnation had been passed." A few days later Dreyfus and Picquart were both restored to the army establishment and promoted. *E pur si muove.*

It should now be possible to form certain conclusions concerning the nature of the crisis through which France had passed. It was certainly "unique, comparable to no other, in that the accused brought the hatred of a whole people not on himself alone but on his whole people," and it is probably true to say that no individual ever wrought so profound a disturbance in the life of a State. "We can take it," says Péguy, truly enough, "as the example, the model, the standard of what is a crisis, an event with its own proper value."

The Dreyfus case, complex as it was in many ways, reduced itself ultimately to a simple choice between the two conceptions of society which had, ever since the Revolution, been struggling for mastery in the French mind: the one, the basing of society and civilization on certain elemental individual rights, which no danger of upheaval or reasons of State could shake in their sanctity, the other based on authority as external and prior to individual citizens, superior to and judge of the rights of these and the desirability of their exercise. It was the Declaration of the Rights of Man versus the *ancien régime,* the Reformation and the Revolution as against the Church, and it suddenly forced every thinking man to choose the side to which he really belonged. "In a very few days each family was at its post, knowing what it was doing, and entrenched behind its closed doors. For Paris has her families no less than Florence, and her unbattlemented walls shelter warring factions. The French mind took up again with startling rapidity its classical points of vantage, the one authoritarian, the other libertarian; the one religious, the other critical. It was swifter and more accurate than deliberate obedience or conscious thought: men of the Right and men of the Left, their movements seemed to outstrip their ideas; for the first time in their lives they found their true position, recognized their true companions. That resurrection of all the pasts of a nation," adds M. Halévy, not without a melancholy humour, "was very significant, but uncomfortable for those whom it gripped." Very uncomfortable indeed, and providing a most satisfactory "moral alternative to war" for the display without bloodshed of all the heroisms that war demands.

The issue, be it said once more, complex and tangled as it seemed, was indeed simple enough, demanding a plain yes or no, leaving no loophole, no room for subtle distinctions; so simple that in fact all the right was bound to be on the one side or other, so that it seemed to realize the rare occurrence in practical life of a real inescapable absolute. Péguy put the dilemma in terms which cannot be bettered: "A nation is something unique, a gigantic assemblage of the most legitimate, the most sacred, rights and interests. Thousands and millions of lives depend on it in the present, the past and the future. . . . It is all of infinite price because it can only be made once, be realized once; it cannot be made or begun over again. . . . The first duty of so unique an achievement is not to let itself be jeopardized for one man, whoever he be, however legitimate his interests; that is a right no nation possesses. That is the language of wisdom, of reason. Dreyfus had to sacrifice himself, and to be sacrificed against his will, if needs be, for the repose, for the safety of France. So some said. But we answered that a single injustice, a single crime, a single illegality, especially if it be officially confirmed and registered, a single insult offered to justice and to right, especially if it be universally, legally, nationally, conveniently accepted, a single crime, is enough to break the whole social pact; a single breach of honour, a single disgraceful act, is enough to dishonour and disgrace a whole nation. It is a gangrenous spot, which soon spreads over the whole body. What we defend is not our honour only, not only the honour of our nation now, but the historic honour of our nation, of our race, the honour of our ancestors, the honour of our children." In one word, adds Péguy, "our adversaries were concerned with the temporal salvation of our country, we were concerned with the salvation of its eternal soul." And with that we must leave it, noting, still with Péguy, that "people will never be able to speak lightly of it."

Vichy: Revenge of the Anti-Dreyfusards

WILHELM HERZOG

Wilhelm Herzog was a German writer who went into exile in 1933 with the coming of Hitler to power. During World War II he escaped from German internment in France, settled eventually in the United States, and returned to Germany only in 1952. He has edited a book containing the newspaper articles written at the time of the Dreyfus Affair and is author of its most detailed study from a socialist viewpoint, *Der Kampf einer Republik*. The last chapter of his work, *From Dreyfus to Pétain*, is entitled, "The Struggle Never Ends," and describes Pétain's rise to power. Herzog calls the Vichy government a "tragic sequel to the Dreyfus Affair," because it was the "belated revenge of the generals for their defeat in the Dreyfus Case." The intensity with which the chapter is written is explained by the author's testimony that he saw with his own eyes "how the old passions, which at the time of the Dreyfus Affair had split France into two camps, were again aroused by the German poison administered under Pétain's ludicrous and brutal dictatorship," and he "began to write this final chapter under the impact of this indelible experience."

I N August, 1945, forty years after the conclusion of the Dreyfus Affair, American newspapers reported from Paris the trial of Maréchal Pétain as fully and with the same passionate interest that they had accorded the trial of Captain Dreyfus four decades ago.

As different as the accused were, the "Victor of Verdun," the "Maréchal de France," the "Savior of France" (or whatever other false titles were bestowed upon him) and this little Jewish officer of the French General Staff for whose acquittal men like Clemenceau, Zola, and Jaurès fought with unswerving passion after he had been innocently convicted in 1894, the political background is the same in both cases. The factions that opposed each other are nearly corresponding, and the dissension which led to the revolution and to the civil war, literally splitting the nation into two camps, is almost uncannily similar. The Parisian press and radio correspondents in the United States reported at the end of the Pétain trial: "The country remains divided as it was after the Dreyfus case. . . ."

That is by no means astonishing.

The French General Staff has never got over the defeat inflicted upon them by the republicans about 1900. They could never forget what was wreaked upon them as a result of the revision of the Dreyfus trial and the subsequent rehabilitation of the Jewish captain whom they had branded as a traitor. In the eyes of France and the whole world they were compromised, shamefully exposed, and charged with major crimes.

Clemenceau referred to them as a pirate's den, a sewer full of dangerous bandits. In his daring pamphlets, he accused the top generals of having debased themselves as accomplices of the real traitor, Major Esterhazy, who delivered to the German military attaché, von Schwartzkoppen, no less than 162 secret documents.

The generals of France at about 1900, the head of the General Staff, Boisdeffre, the Minister of War, Mercier, and General

Pellieux permitted the conviction of an innocent man and assumed a protective attitude toward the real traitor, the spy who called himself Count Walsin-Esterhazy. In 1940, Maréchal Pétain had General de Gaulle sentenced to death for treason, while he himself concluded a truce with France's mortal enemy and condescended to become Hitler's collaborator, thus betraying the Allies. For four long years he was extolled as a great patriot by his venal and sycophantic followers. The most dubious and corrupt politicians became his closest assistants. He appointed such men as Laval, Flandin, and Déat ministers, men who wanted to do business with Hitler and Mussolini long before the outbreak of World War II.

Just what induced this general, who had become gray while serving his country honorably and upon whom the dignity of a Maréchal was conferred in the Third Republic, to ally himself with these notorious traitors and henchmen of the dictators? It was not only his defeatism, of which he gave such unmistakable evidence even in World War I, but primarily his hatred for the Republic, for whose downfall he longed and strove; exactly like General Boulanger in 1889; like the generals at the time of the Dreyfus Affair. Where they had failed, he thought he would succeed; all the more, as he had carefully prepared his plan which he kept secret for a long time. As an old reactionary, he believed in the power of the dictatorships. In Italy, Germany, Spain, Portugal, Poland, Hungary, and in the Balkan countries, the democratic governments were abolished by force. Dictatorship came from within as the dawn of the fascist era.

The attempts of the French nationalistic movements — *Croix de feu* and *Cagoulards* — which had evolved, following the pattern of the German Nazis and the Italian Fascists, to establish a dictatorship in France, were foiled in 1936. Pétain remained in the background and bided his time. Despite his advanced years, the ambitious marshal anticipated the realization of his dreams.

But how were they to be realized? If not from within by means of a national revolution, then from without, even at the price of defeat by the German archenemy. Pétain was already a long-standing fascist when the democratic Republic chose him as generalissimo (1919–1931) and even made him Minister of War in 1934!

It seems to be the destiny of most young republics to have their armies commanded by generals supposedly disinterested in politics but who from the bottom of their hearts are mortal enemies of democracy and republican administration. This was the case in France, in Germany, and in Spain.

Forty years ago Pétain's part was played by Boisdeffre and Mercier. Graduates of the Jesuit Military Academy of Saint Cyr, who became members of the General Staff, were often talented military scientists as well as devout Catholics and staunch reactionaries. They formed a caste, in fact a state within the state, responsible only to their militaristic superiors.

Secluded, isolated, and invested with great power, these despotic autocrats ruled their nation with force while being acclaimed as guardians of tradition. Regardless of whether they chalked up victories, suffered defeats, or never had the opportunity of proving their strategic talent, they were venerated as demigods. The newspapers and magazines, especially those ill-disposed toward the Republic, liked to display their pictures ostentatiously, accompanied by high-flown praise.

Even the Republic itself surrounded them with an aura of heroism, dressed them in magnificent uniforms and colorful dresscoats covered with medals and gold braid, paid them extravagantly, and allowed them full power and control in their department, in most cases not even checking on their activities.

It would be unfair to hold the generals solely responsible for all the misfortune which befell the Third Republic. The

three great affairs between 1889 and 1906
— Boulanger's coup d'état, designed to
overthrow the Republic and to establish a
dictatorship, the Panama scandal, and the
Dreyfus Affair — were caused by the
weakness of the Republic, its rottenness,
and its corrupt favoritism. . . .

Pétain felt chosen to act on orders and
on behalf of the ruling class, of all privi-
leged by birth and property. Indeed, he was
also the exponent of the aristocratic military dignitaries, of the Catholic clergy, and
of the capitalistic group which was closely
connected with it; that group which made
its press, the master of "public opinion,"
proclaim that the Republic was diving into
an abyss.

This gave the dictatorship its start. The
marshal had gone to work with far greater
circumspection than his predecessor, General Boulanger, cleverer and surer of what
he was doing than the generals at the time
of the Panama scandal and the Dreyfus
Affair. They all had advanced too soon;
this was not the marshal's way. They too
had powerful protectors and zealous servants, but the blow with which they struck
against the Republic remained unsuc-
cessful.

Pétain, the theorist and practitioner of
defeatism, was successful. He did not un-
dertake his coup d'état during peace time,
but in the midst of a war and, so to speak,
in a lawful way. Had not the representatives chosen by the people helped him
legally to seize power, him who bore the
main responsibility for the military catastrophe? Did not their forefathers choose
Maréchal MacMahon, who was beaten at
Sedan, to be President of the Republic?
Did not the German republicans after
World War I twice elect the beaten Field
Marshal von Hindenburg their president
of the Reich, in 1932 as well as in 1925?

Obviously it is the marshals of the over-
thrown regimes who are predestined to
head republics time and again. Inciden-
tally, the similarity between these two old
men is amazing. Both of them, the "Victor
of Tannenberg" (which he was not) and

the "Victor of Verdun" (which he was
not), came from the old school. They were
staunch reactionaries and nationalists, but
were considered honorable men who would
never break their allegiance to the Republic, and both world-famous figures be-
trayed their Republics.

However, they differed from each other
in one thing: Pétain, the type of the old
general who had been born during the
Second Empire and who, as a boy, admired
Napoleon III, respected the Third French
Republic *nolens volens* as much as Hindenburg respected the Weimar Republic. But
the Maréchal of France had set his aim
even higher than that East Prussian. He
wanted to be not only the iron Hindenburg, but also the Hitler, of France.

The ideas he lacked were supplied to
him by his old friend Charles Maurras, the
most important ideologist of the counterrevolution and the head of the royalists
and superpatriots for many decades. However, what mainly stimulated Pétain, who
did not lay much stress on ideas, to imi-
tate Hitler's methods was the idea of up-
holding the authority and mastery of one
stratum, of one race, or of the so-called
elite of society. The fanatic reactionary,
loathing from the bottom of his heart
everything that was democratic, was de-
lighted not only by the magnificent parades, the goose-stepping battalions of
brown and black shirts, the blind obedience, the uniformed masses of men, but
particularly by the absolute commanding
power of the "Fuehrer."

He hoped that through such means, and
only through such, France, poisoned with
the ideas of the Revolution of 1789 and
the establishment of the Republic, would
be "cured" and would find her way back
to the monarchy.

Pétain, who had gained the highest rank
and honors in this Republic, was the son
of peasants from the village Cauchy-a-la-
Tour in the Pas-de-Calais Department and
received a scholarship from the Jesuits. He
remained a secret royalist all his life, a
pious Catholic, an enemy of the workers

in the cities, and a violent counterrevolutionary. His carriage and his overbearing attitude were determined not only by his rustic origin and his education in a Jesuitic school and later in the feudal Military Academy at Saint-Cyr, but also by his individual insensitivity, his indifference and arrogance, which he revealed time and again in the narrow-minded horizon of the professional soldier. He was the typical general of the "ancien régime" in the Third Republic, without imagination, but ambitious and tenacious in his basically conservative outlook on life. . . .

According to those who stormed the Bastille, there were "inalienable rights." Well, he alienated them. He had millions of Frenchmen deported to Germany as slave workers. He had French, German, Belgian, and Austrian Jews, who had escaped into the then still unoccupied zone of France, persecuted, arrested, tortured, starved to death, and gassed. He converted the judiciary into a public whore. He handed over anti-Hitler politicians, German and French alike, to the Gestapo. They had been kept behind barbed wire for years; they were mentally and often also physically maltreated.

He arrested and murdered his personal antagonists, such men as the former Minister of the Interior, Dormoy, who held in his hands the documentary proof of the marshal's relation to the *Cagoulards,* and Georges Mandel, the Minister of the Interior in the cabinet of Reynaud, who opposed the capitulation. He had completely innocent people shot as hostages. Countless are the infamous crimes against defenseless people who were exposed to the most shameless police system. The brutal treatment of the heroes of the Maquis, the real patriots, surpassed Louis XIV's dragonnades against the French Protestants. The fighters of the resistance movement were baited like hunted game, they were spied on, trapped, exposed to the meanest tortures, poisoned, crushed, or shot without any trial by Pétain's militia, whose leadership was in the hands of a notorious criminal.

Such was the result of four years of Pétain's dictatorship. What had it to set against the ideals of 1789? Submission against freedom, the *Gleichshaltung,* according to the German image, against equality, the hatred of Frenchmen against fraternity among themselves. The whole of France had become a Bastille again. It was erected by the "Savior of France" to enable him to master as autocrat the freest and liveliest intellects in Europe and to fit them into the "new order" of dictatorships. The old reactionary — the word "revolution" made him shudder — had to camouflage his counterrevolution as a "national revolution."

The pitiable old man thought that he would finally succeed, together with Hitler and Mussolini, who had introduced the new fascist epoch of world history, in liquidating the ideas of 1789, which he had hated from early childhood. . . .

France's tragedy in 1940 was that there were no such men as Clemenceau, Zola, or Jaurès, who, during the Dreyfus Affair, were farsighted, active, politically unswerving enough to take up the fight against reaction and the high generals. Under Clemenceau, no Pétain could ever have seized power. He would have sent the "Maréchal de France" where he had sent General Boulanger, who had also risen high because of his popularity. A Laval would have crept into hiding; he could never have played his rôle of the villain and pimp without being unmasked in time.

But Daladier, Reynaud, and even Léon Blum were helpless before the immense danger. They were unable to cope with this situation. So they let the flag of the Republic be hauled down. No historian of this disgraceful period in the history of France will be able to suppress the fact that 395 deputies voted for the change of the constitution as demanded by Pétain and only 3 against it.

One man, however, seized the flag and held it high again. This audacious standard-

bearer, Charles de Gaulle, became the symbol of that France which continued the
struggle. Like Colonel Picquart, the only
officer who testified in public to Dreyfus'
innocence, de Gaulle, the colonel, who had
just then been advanced to the rank of a
general, uncovered the lie, the hypocrisy,
and the treachery of the other generals
who suddenly became ardent pacifists. In
the same way that Picquart felt the injustice and the crimes committed by the General Staff a disgrace to the French army,
Pétain's and Weygand's miserable maso-
chistic submission was unbearable for de
Gaulle who, at that time, did not know the
political motives of these men. . . .

The sovereignty of the generals was a
sacred tradition in Germany and in the
France of the Third Republic, which, despite its republican façade, permitted its
generals to lead a unique existence, enthroned above the people. Thanks to
Clemenceau's powerful leadership, a
change in this respect occurred, even in
the midst of a war. Such excellent army
leaders as Joffre and Foch felt it. But it
was only a passing period. And soon again,
the French General Staff existed as a state
within a state. They hurriedly reconquered
their lost power because of the weakness
of the republican ministers. Generals remain what they are: the representatives of
their caste.

De Gaulle, Weygand, and Pétain are
the successors of Mercier, Boisdeffre, Pellieux, Billot, and Zurlinden, of the Dreyfus Affair, not only because of their positions as officers on the General Staff, but
also because of their spirit. They may have
different faces, one may be cleverer or more
educated than the other, but their uniform
and tradition, their conception of their military mission, their admiration for aristocracy, identify them all. The opportunistic
ministers, the political publicists, and the
undiscerning critics must be blamed for
generals gaining popularity. Those men
who shape public opinion, who should en-
lighten the people and who also are capable
of doing so, since they knew Pétain's and

Weygand's past, those men remain silent
and thus help to spread the legends and
fairy tales about the glory of these enemies
of the people.

Paul Reynaud, the last Prime Minister
of the Third Republic and Pétain's immediate predecessor, confessed that he left
Pétain's reputation untouched against his
better judgment. "Because I thought," he
wrote in his diary, "that the French people
would need men to whom they can look
up, I prevented the publication of certain
files, up to two years before the outbreak
of the war, which would have exposed
Maréchal Pétain." He did not even seem to
notice how much he exposed himself with
such a statement. Now after the great
catastrophe, France's collapse, the loss of
millions of her best sons and the dying of
women and children, he confessed the
truth which he withheld from the people.
As all the other initiated, he kept it a
secret so that the prestige of the "Victor of
Verdun" should not suffer, but grow instead, because one has to preserve false
gods for the people rather than none at all.

The truth about Pétain was not allowed
to come to light, the General Staff was
untouchable, exactly as in the days of the
Dreyfus Affair. How much unspeakable
suffering could Reynaud, Daladier, and
Léon Blum have spared France had they
unveiled this idol sooner!

The causes of the catastrophe rest here
and not in the decadence of the people.
The causes are more strongly rooted in
moral than in political and military issues.
The conventional lies, the self-evident hypocrisy, the false comradeship among those
political leaders who knew everything and
remained silent about it, that was the main
evil in the Third Republic, one of its
most dangerous diseases which it never
overcame despite the Panama scandal and
the Dreyfus Affair. . . .

During the Pétain regime this cleavage
[between conservative and radical France]
was still crasser; all anti-Dreyfusards were
pro-Vichy and all Dreyfusards against
Vichy. Such men as Édouard Herriot and

Léon Blum stood in the front row of the Dreyfusards; Maréchal Pétain, at that time detached as a captain to the Military Governor of Paris, General Zurlinden, one of the most violent anti-Dreyfusards, totally shared the general's opinion, according to his own statement. The demarcation line between the two hostile camps is therefore very old. One can say it is sacred through tradition and struggles.

A Preview of Twentieth-Century Totalitarianism

HANNAH ARENDT

Hannah Arendt received her Ph.D. from the University of Heidelberg at the age of twenty-two and also has the distinction of being the only woman ever appointed full professor at Princeton University. In *The Origins of Totalitarianism*, from which the following passages are taken, she attempts to trace the roots of two twentieth-century totalitarian systems, Nazism and Communism, in the anti-semitism and imperialism of the nineteenth century.

WHILE the Dreyfus Affair in its broader political aspects belongs to the twentieth century, the Dreyfus case, the various trials of the Jewish Captain Alfred Dreyfus, are quite typical of the nineteenth century, when men followed legal proceedings so keenly because each instance afforded a test of the century's greatest achievement, the complete impartiality of the law. It is characteristic of the period that a miscarriage of justice could arouse such political passions and inspire such an endless succession of trials and retrials, not to speak of duels and fisticuffs. The doctrine of equality before the law was still so firmly implanted in the conscience of the civilized world that a single miscarriage of justice could provoke public indignation from Moscow to New York. Nor was anyone, except in France itself, so "modern" as to associate the matter with political issues. The wrong done to a single Jewish officer in France was able to draw from the rest of the world a more vehement and united reaction than all the persecutions of German Jews a generation later. Even Czarist Russia could accuse France of barbarism, while in Germany members of the Kaiser's entourage would openly express an indignation matched only by the radical press of the 1930's.

The *dramatis personae* of the case might have stepped out of the pages of Balzac: on the one hand, the class-conscious generals frantically covering up for the members of their own clique and, on the other, their antagonist, Picquart, with his calm, clear-eyed and slightly ironical honesty. Beside them stand the nondescript crowd of the men in Parliament, each terrified of what his neighbor might know; the President of the Republic, notorious patron of the Paris brothels, and the examining magistrates, living solely for the sake of social contacts. Then there is Dreyfus himself, actually a parvenu, continually boasting to his colleagues of his family fortune which he spent on women; his brothers, pathetically offering their entire fortune, and then reducing the offer to 150,000 francs, for the release of their kinsman, never quite sure whether they wished to make a sacrifice or simply to suborn the General Staff; and the lawyer Démange, really convinced of his client's innocence but basing the defense on an issue of doubt so as to save himself from attacks and injury to his personal interests. Lastly, there is the adventurer Esterhazy, he of the ancient escutcheon, so utterly bored by this bourgeois world as to seek relief equally in heroism and knavery. An erstwhile second lieutenant of the Foreign Legion, he impressed his colleagues greatly by his superior boldness and impudence. Always in trouble, he lived by serving as duelist's second to Jewish officers and by blackmailing their wealthy coreligionists. Indeed, he would avail himself of the good offices of the chief rabbi himself in order to obtain the requisite introductions. Even in his ultimate downfall he remained true to the Balzac tradition. Not treason nor wild dreams of a great orgy in which a hundred thousand besotted Prussian Uhlans would run berserk through Paris, but a paltry embezzlement of a relative's cash sent him to his doom. And what shall we say of Zola, with his impassioned moral fervor, his somewhat empty pathos, and his melodramatic declaration, on the eve of his flight to London, that he had heard the voice of Dreyfus begging him to bring this sacrifice?

All this belongs typically to the nineteenth century and by itself would never have survived two World Wars. The old-time enthusiasm of the mob for Esterhazy, like its hatred of Zola, have long since died down to embers, but so too has that fiery passion against aristocracy and clergy which had once inflamed Jaurès and which had alone secured the final release of Dreyfus. As the Cagoulard affair was to show, officers of the General Staff no longer had to fear the wrath of the people when they hatched their plots for a *coup d'état*. Since the separation of Church and State, France, though certainly no longer clerical-minded, had lost a great deal of her anticlerical feeling, just as the Catholic Church had itself lost much of its political aspiration. Pétain's attempt to convert the republic into a Catholic state was blocked by the utter indifference of the people and by the lower clergy's hostility to clerico-fascism.

The Dreyfus Affair in its political implications could survive because two of its elements grew in importance during the twentieth century. The first is hatred of the Jews; the second, suspicion of the republic itself, of Parliament, and the state machine. The larger section of the public could still go on thinking the latter, rightly or wrongly, under the influence of the Jews and the power of the banks. Down to our times the term Anti-Dreyfusard can still serve as a recognized name for all that is antirepublican, antidemocratic, and antisemitic. A few years ago it still comprised everything, from the monarchism of the Action Française to the National Bolshevism of Doriot and the social Fascism of Déat. It was not, however, to these Fascist groups, numerically unimportant as they were, that the Third Republic owed its collapse. On the contrary, the plain, if paradoxical, truth is that their influence was never so slight as at the moment when the collapse actually took place. What made France fall was the fact that she had no more true Dreyfusards, no one who believed that democracy and freedom, equality and justice could any longer be defended or realized under the republic. At long last the republic fell like overripe fruit into the lap of that old Anti-Dreyfusard clique which had always formed the kernel of her army, and this at a time when she had few enemies but almost no friends. How little the Pétain clique was a product of German Fascism was shown clearly by its slavish adherence to the old formulas of forty years before.

While Germany shrewdly truncated her and ruined her entire economy through the demarcation line, France's leaders in Vichy tinkered with the old Barrès formula of "autonomous provinces," thereby crippling her all the more. They introduced anti-Jewish legislation more promptly than any Quisling, boasting all the while that they had no need to import antisemitism from Germany and that their law governing the Jews differed in essential points from that of the Reich. They sought to mobilize the Catholic clergy against the Jews, only to give proof that the priests have not only lost their political influence, but are not actually antisemites. On the contrary, it was the very bishops and synods which the Vichy regime wanted to turn once more into political powers who voiced the most emphastic protest against the persecution of the Jews.

Not the Dreyfus case with its trials but the Dreyfus Affair in its entirety offers a foregleam of the twentieth century. As Bernanos pointed out in 1931, "The Dreyfus affair already belongs to that tragic era which certainly was not ended by the last war. The affair reveals the same inhuman character, preserving amid the welter of unbridled passions and the flames of hate an inconceivably cold and callous heart." Certainly it was not in France that the true sequel to the affair was to be found, but the reason why France fell an easy prey to Nazi aggression is not far to seek. Hitler's propaganda spoke a language long familiar and never quite forgotten. That the "Caesarism" of the *Action Française* and the nihilistic nationalism of Barrès and Maurras never succeeded in their original form is due to a variety of causes, all of them negative. They lacked social vision and were unable to translate into popular terms those mental phantasmagoria which their contempt for the intellect had engendered.

We are here concerned essentially with the political bearings of the Dreyfus Affair and not with the legal aspects of the case. Sharply outlined in it are a number of traits characteristic of the twentieth century. Faint and barely distinguishable during the early decades of the century, they have at last emerged into full daylight and stand revealed as belonging to the main trends of modern times. After thirty years of a mild, purely social form of anti-Jewish discrimination, it had become a little difficult to remember that the cry, "Death to the Jews," had echoed through the length and breadth of a modern state once before when its domestic policy was crystallized in the issue of antisemitism. For thirty years the old legends of world conspiracy had been no more than the conventional stand-by of the tabloid press and the dime novel and the world did not easily remember that not long ago, but at a time when the "Protocols of the Elders of Zion" were still unknown, a whole nation had been racking its brains trying to determine whether "secret Rome" or "secret Judah" held the reins of world politics.

Similarly, the vehement and nihilistic philosophy of spiritual self-hatred suffered something of an eclipse when a world at temporary peace with itself yielded no crop of outstanding criminals to justify the exaltation of brutality and unscrupulousness. The Jules Guérins had to wait nearly forty years before the atmosphere was ripe again for quasi-military storm troops. The *déclassés,* produced through nineteenth-century economy, had to grow numerically until they were strong minorities of the nations, before that *coup d'état,* which had remained but a grotesque plot in France, could achieve reality in Germany almost without effort. The prelude to Nazism was played over the entire European stage. The Dreyfus case, therefore, is more than a bizarre, imperfectly solved "crime," an affair of staff officers disguised by false beards and dark glasses, peddling their stupid forgeries by night in the streets of Paris. Its hero is not Dreyfus but Clemenceau, and it begins not with the arrest of a Jewish staff officer but with the Panama scandal. . . .

So long as there was only the Dreyfus family trying with bizarre methods to rescue their kinsman from Devil's Island, and so long as there were only Jews concerned about their standing in the antisemitic salons and the still more antisemitic army, everything certainly pointed that way [toward a bloodless *coup d'état*]. Obviously there was no reason to expect an attack on the army or on society from *that* quarter. Was not the sole desire of the Jews to continue to be accepted in society and suffered in the armed forces? No one in military or civilian circles needed to suffer a sleepless night on *their* account. It was disconcerting, therefore, when it transpired that in the intelligence office of the General Staff there sat a high officer, who, though possessed of a good Catholic background, excellent military prospects, and the "proper" degree of antipathy toward the Jews, had yet not adopted the principle that the end justifies the means. Such a man, utterly divorced from social clannishness or professional ambition, was Picquart, and of this simple, quiet, politically disinterested spirit the General Staff was soon to have its fill. Picquart was no hero and certainly no martyr. He was simply that common type of citizen with an average interest in public affairs who in the hour of danger (though not a minute earlier) stands up to defend his country in the same unquestioning way as he discharges his daily duties. Nevertheless, the cause only grew serious when, after several delays and hesitations, Clemenceau at last became convinced that Dreyfus was innocent and the republic in danger. At the beginning of the struggle only a handful of well-known writers and scholars rallied to the cause—Zola; Anatole France; E. Duclaux; Gabriel Monod, the historian; and Lucien Herr, librarian of the École Normale. To these must be added the small and then insignificant circle of young intellectuals who were later to make history in the *Cahiers de la quinzaine.* That, however, was the full roster of Clemenceau's allies. There was no political group, not a single politician of repute, ready to stand at his side. The greatness of Clemenceau's approach lies in the fact that it was not directed against a particular miscarriage of justice, but was based upon such "abstract" ideas as justice, liberty, and civic virtue. It was based, in short, on those very concepts which had formed the staple of old-time Jacobin patriotism and against which much mud and abuse had already been hurled. As time wore on and Clemenceau continued, unmoved by threats and disappointments, to enunciate the same truths and to embody them in demands, the more "concrete" nationalists lost ground. Followers of men like Barrès, who had accused the supporters of Dreyfus of losing themselves in a "welter of metaphysics," came to realize that the abstractions of the "Tiger" were actually nearer to political realities than the limited intelligence of ruined businessmen or the barren traditionalism of fatalistic intellectuals. Where the concrete approach of the realistic nationalists eventually led them is illustrated by the priceless story of how Charles Maurras had "the honor and pleasure," after the defeat of France, of falling in during his flight to the south with a female astrologer who interpreted to him the political meaning of recent events and advised him to collaborate with the Nazis.

Although antisemitism had undoubtedly gained ground during the three years following the arrest of Dreyfus, before the opening of Clemenceau's campaign, and although the anti-Jewish press had attained a circulation comparable to that of the chief papers, the streets had remained quiet. It was only when Clemenceau began his articles in *L'Aurore,* when Zola published his *J'Accuse,* and when the Rennes tribunal set off the dismal succession of trials and retrials that the mob stirred into action. Every stroke of the Dreyfusards (who were known to be a small minority) was followed by a more or less violent disturbance on the streets. The organization of the mob by the General Staff was remarkable. The trail leads straight from the army to the *Libre Parole* which, directly or indirectly, through its articles or the personal intervention of its editors, mobilized students, monarchists, adventurers, and plain gangsters and pushed them into the streets. If Zola uttered a word, at once his windows were stoned. If Scheurer-Kestner wrote to the colonial minister, he was at once beaten up on the streets while the papers made scurrilous attacks on his private life. And all accounts agree that if Zola, when once charged, had been acquitted he would never have left the courtroom alive.

The cry, "Death to the Jews," swept the country. In Lyon, Rennes, Nantes, Tours, Bordeaux, Clermont-Ferrand, and Marseille — everywhere, in fact — antisemitic riots broke out and were invariably traceable to the same source. Popular indignation broke out everywhere on the same day and at precisely the same hour. Under the leadership of Guérin the mob took on a military complexion. Antisemitic shock troops appeared on the streets and made certain that every pro-Dreyfus meeting should end in bloodshed. The complicity of the police was everywhere patent.

The most modern figure on the side of the Anti-Dreyfusards was probably Jules Guérin. Ruined in business, he had begun his political career as a police stool pigeon, and acquired that flair for discipline and organization which invariably marks the underworld. This he was later able to divert into political channels, becoming the founder and head of the Ligue Antisémite. In him high society found its first criminal hero. In its adulation of Guérin bourgeois society showed clearly that in its code of morals and ethics it had broken for good with its own standards. Behind the Ligue stood two members of the aristocracy, the Duke of Orléans and the Marquis de Morès. The latter had lost his fortune in America and become famous for organizing the butchers of Paris into a manslaughtering brigade.

Most eloquent of these modern tendencies was the farcical siege of the so-called Fort Chabrol. It was here, in this first of "Brown Houses," that the cream of the Ligue Antisémite foregathered when the police decided at last to arrest their leader. The installations were the acme of technical perfection. "The windows were protected by iron shutters. There was a system of electric bells and telephones from cellar to roof. Five yards or so behind the massive entrance, itself always kept locked and bolted, there was a tall grill of cast iron. On the right, between the grill and the main entrance was a small door, likewise

iron-plated, behind which sentries, handpicked from the butcher legions, mounted guard day and night." Max Régis, instigator of the Algerian pogroms, is another who strikes a modern note. It was this youthful Régis who once called upon a cheering Paris rabble to "water the tree of freedom with the blood of the Jews." Régis represented that section of the movement which hoped to achieve power by legal and parliamentary methods. In accordance with this program he had himself elected mayor of Algiers and utilized his office to unleash the pogroms in which several Jews were killed, Jewish women criminally assaulted, and Jewish-owned stores looted. It was to him also that the polished and cultured Édouard Drumont, that most famous French antisemite, owed his seat in Parliament.

What was new in all this was not the activity of the mob; for that there were abundant precedents. What was new and surprising at the time — though all too familiar to us — was the organization of the mob and the hero-worship enjoyed by its leaders. The mob became the direct agent of that "concrete" nationalism espoused by Barrès, Maurras, and Daudet, who together formed what was undoubtedly a kind of elite of the younger intellectuals. These men, who despised the people and who had themselves but recently emerged from a ruinous and decadent cult of estheticism, saw in the mob a living expression of virile and primitive "strength." It was they and their theories which first identified the mob with the people and converted its leaders into national heroes. It was their philosophy of pessimism and their delight in doom that was the first sign of the imminent collapse of the European intelligentsia.

SUGGESTIONS FOR ADDITIONAL READING

Because of the countless polemics and interminable testimony and political debates, as well as the swarm of writers, politicians, and others capable of setting forth their views in endless books, articles, and pamphlets, a bibliography of material on the Dreyfus Affair would alone fill a volume of at least this size. The suggestions that follow, therefore, will necessarily be very selective.

A familiarity with the pre-1914 political, social, and economic developments of the Third French Republic is obviously indispensable for an understanding of the Affair. Several good and basic histories may be found listed in the appropriate section, edited by Lynn M. Case and Jean Stengers, of the American Historical Association's *Guide to Historical Literature* (Washington, 1961). You should make sure to get as wide a sampling as possible, moving from historians like Bainville, on the right, to Zévaès, on the left.

Next, you should consult bibliographies of works on the Affair. As early as 1905 a good one, already containing 728 titles, was compiled by Paul Desachy, *Bibliographie de l'Affaire Dreyfus* (Paris, 1905). More recent and detailed bibliographies may be found in the 1938 edition of Dutrait-Crozon, *Précis de l'Affaire Dreyfus* (Paris, 1938), and in Louis Leblois, *L'Affaire Dreyfus: L'Iniquité, La Réparation, Les Principaux Faits et Les Principaux Documents* (Paris, 1929). The second book is especially useful as an outline in which the important documents are analyzed in context. The French edition of Jacques Kayser, *L'Affaire Dreyfus* (Paris, 1946), also lists the principal documents available.

Among the general histories of the Affair, those quoted in this volume ought to be included in any additional reading. We have seen excerpts only from Volume I of Reinach's history; there are seven volumes all told and although more information has appeared since their publication, they are still excellent. The Dutrait-Crozon and Leblois books are cited above. Leblois was Picquart's lawyer and friend, and his revisionist views also provide a good antidote to those of Dutrait-Crozon and Bainville. Some other histories worthy of mention are Armand Charpentier, *Historique de l'Affaire Dreyfus* (Paris, 1933), English translation, 1935 (The French version contains facsimiles of the chief documents); Bruno Weil, *Der Prozess des Hauptmanns Dreyfus* (Berlin, 1930); Theodore Reinach, *Histoire sommaire de l'Affaire Dreyfus* (Paris, 1924); and Pierre Miquel, *L'Affaire Dreyfus* (Paris, 1959). Charpentier's *Les Côtés mystérieux de l'Affaire Dreyfus* (Paris, 1937), offers the thesis that Esterhazy wrote the *bordereau* at the orders and under the dictation of Colonel Sandherr. New life is breathed into the "third man" thesis by Maurice Paléologue, who acted as liaison between the Foreign Office and the General Staff, and whose posthumous memoirs, *Journal de l'Affaire Dreyfus* (Paris, 1955), recently created a stir, and by Henri Giscard d'Estaing, *D'Esterhazy à Dreyfus* (Paris, 1960). The latter tries to show that the "third man" insisted on, but unnamed by Paléologue, was Mercier himself. (There is a discussion of these books and the entire thesis in an appendix to Marcel Thomas, *L'Affaire sans Dreyfus* (Paris, 1961). Robert F. Byrnes, *Antisemitism in Modern France* (New Brunswick, 1950), provides important background material but the volume, one of two projected, ends just before Dreyfus' arrest.

Students who wish to consult works appearing at the time for or against revision should consult those by Barrès, Clemenceau, Jaurès, Yvès Guyot, Joseph Reinach, Zola, and Lazare. Other names and titles may be found in the bibliography in Jacques Kayser, mentioned above.

Personal letters and memoirs of the leading actors should also be looked at. Dreyfus' own memoirs of the years spent on

Devil's Island appeared in 1901 under the title of *Cinq Années de ma vie, 1894–1899* (Paris, 1901), of which there is an English translation. In 1936 there appeared Dreyfus' memoirs from 1899 to 1906 and in the same volume an attempt by his son to tell the story from 1859–1894, and 1906–1935 (the last being the year of Dreyfus' death)—*Souvenirs et Correspondance publiés par son fils* (Paris, 1936). Samplings from these two books are found in Donald McDay, *The Dreyfus Case. By the man — Alfred Dreyfus — and his son — Pierre Dreyfus* (New Haven, 1937). The memoirs of Maurice Barrès appeared as *Mes Cahiers*, Volume I (1896–98), in 1929, II (1898–1902), in 1930, and III, IV, in 1931. Charles Péguy published his *Notre Jeunesse* in 1910.

Biographies of prominent Frenchmen of the period describe their participation in the Affair. There are many of Jaurès; the latest and best is that of Harvey Goldberg, *The Life of Jaurès* (Madison, 1962). One of Clemenceau is by Geoffrey Brunn, *Clemenceau* (Cambridge, 1943); and one of Zola by Matthew Josephson, *Zola and His Time* (N.Y., 1928).

One source, most useful in describing the prevailing climate of opinion, is the novel. Roger Martin du Gard's *Jean Barois* is unsurpassed here. An English translation was published in New York in 1949.

Other works include the trilogy of Maurice Barrès, *Les Déracinés, L'Appel au soldat,* and *Leurs figures;* Émile Zola, *Vérité;* and the volumes of Marcel Proust, *Remembrance of Things Past.*

Newspapers and reviews are especially useful, both as sources of information and as guides to opinion in the revisionist and anti-revisionist camps. *La Croix* and *La Libre Parole* were notoriously anti-Dreyfusard; *Le Figaro* became Dreyfusard, as did *La Petite République*, the leading socialist newspaper of the period. To see how the other newspapers took sides and for a description of their role in the Affair, see Raymond Manevy, *La Presse de la IIIe République* (Paris, 1955). More objective — and more impressionistic — accounts may be found in the monthly and bi-monthly *revues*. Among others, *La Revue des Deux Mondes, La Nouvelle Revue, La Revue Socialiste,* and *La Revue Politique et Parlementaire* may be mentioned. The last contained an especially good news summary.

Finally, those interested in archival and manuscript sources should consult the list of archival materials contained in the bibliography of Marcel Thomas, *L'Affaire sans Dreyfus;* and refer to Maurice Baumont, *Aux Sources de l'Affaire Dreyfus, L'Affaire Dreyfus d'après les Archives diplomatiques* (Paris, 1959).